By Faith . . .
I'm Still Standing

Go climb your mountain!

Psalm 73:28

Al Argister

By Faith . . .

I'm Still Standing

Triumph over paralysis

Al Higginbotham

with foreword by

Jeb Bush

Successful Concepts

ISBN: 0-9713051-0-2
Library of Congress Control Number: 2001-126655

Cover design: Pearl & Associates
Front cover photo: Devon Higginbotham
Typesetting, design and production: Tabby House
Printed in the United States of America

Note: Many names have been changed to protect the privacy
of individuals.

Successful Concepts
P.O. Box 2123
Plant City, FL 33564

Acknowledgments

- **Shepherd Center**—Many times I have told families, if they are ever faced with the situation my family faced in 1995, "Shepherd is the place to go if something bad *like this* happens to you. I am forever grateful to the dedicated staff members for all their work in helping me get on with my life."

- **Keith Kolakowski**—God answered prayers the day he came into my life. Keith treated me as if I was special, but since I left physical therapy treatment, I have learned that he treats *all* people as if they were special.

- **Allen and Kaylon**—My children who bring me such pride and joy. Their wit and spunk help me every day.

- **Fred Johnson**—Thanks for your visit on my first day home, when you shared the faith and said, "I will make the trek to the glacier with you."

- **Dad**—Thank you for your faith and prayers, not only since my accident, but all my life.

Contents

Dedication

I knew there was something special about Devon Brown the day I met her in 1977. Her combination of beauty, intelligence and confidence was like nothing I had seen before.

I wanted to ask her out, but knew she would decline. This was one of those moments in life that I have always wondered *what if I hadn't asked*. But I did, and to my surprise, she accepted.

Two years later we married and our vows included "for better or worse" and "until death do us part." We were committed to one another, but the for *better or worse* part was put to the test after my accident.

God could not have directed me to a more wonderful wife and lifetime companion. Devon is my earthly guardian angel. She was always at my side during the most difficult and trying times. Through all the challenges, our children always knew Mom was there for them as well. I could not have made it without her.

I love you, Devon.

Foreword

One of the really great things about being in public life is spending time with extraordinary people. Through large events and one-on-one conversations, from all across Florida and from around the nation, I've been privileged to hear the stories of so many people who have led and are leading extraordinary lives. Despite the cynicism with which many of us view politics, I'm continually amazed at how often people of quality and character are drawn to it. More than once I've left an event thinking someone has just shared a compelling story full of insight into our common human experience. "That guy should write a book," I'd say to myself.

And now one of them has. Al Higginbotham is a man I'm proud to call my friend, and whose story would be captivating to me based on that friendship alone. But the intimate and personal story Al shares in the following pages, I think, will resonate with many people who have never met him but who will be moved by his words.

Part of the reason for that is the words themselves. They are straightforward and honest, like the man himself. There are real feelings and real pain described here, and he doesn't sugarcoat it. There are also real insights and real wisdom here, and he doesn't embellish it. In reading you'll learn some of Al's philosophy, which is not the kind you get by reading philosophy books.

It's a philosophy about family, about spouses and children and parents. It's a philosophy about the outdoors, about mornings and woods and dirt roads. It's a philosophy about moving—with great difficulty—first from a bed to a chair, then from helplessness to renewed strength and confidence, and ultimately from Hillsborough County, Florida, to a beautiful lake at the top of a mountain in Glacier National Park.

Along the way Al faces the stark reality that life does not prepare us for everything that it has in store. Not everybody experiences that reality in the same way Al has, but we all experience it one way or another, sooner or later. We come to a place that forces us to throw all of our plans, all of our ideas and all of our desires out the window. We come to a place where something that could never happen to us, happens to us.

The truly fortunate among us find in that place what Al found, and that is God. His story reminds us that you don't necessarily have to be looking for God to find Him, or rather for Him to find you. It's both incredibly shocking and incredibly comforting to realize that God has been there all along. And when you start counting on the fact that God will be there all along in the future, that's when faith grows and the most exciting part of life really begins.

JEB BUSH
Governor of Florida
August 2001

CHAPTER 1

A Struggling Dad

Moreover no man knows when his time will come . . .
—Ecclesiastes 9:12

In 1995 I found myself caught in a trap familiar to many parents. I was traveling too much and working long hours as I tried to fulfill the material needs of my family.

Devon and I had been married since 1979 and had two wonderful children, Allen III, and Kaylon Elizabeth, ten and eight years old respectively. They were well-adjusted children attending a private Christian school not far from our home. We had a great marriage. I had excelled early in life in both business and politics. As far as I was concerned, life was in a successful fast lane and set on cruise control. I thought nothing could go wrong, but that was about to change.

I was faced once again with the choice of spending the weekend with my wife and children or going on a business/pleasure trip. I was hesitant, very hesitant, about leaving for the weekend, and told Devon I was going to cancel the trip. But a call from one of my partners in the family agriculture/utility contracting business changed any thoughts of backing out of the hunting trip.

On January 18, 1995, Allen and I were headed to the mall. I had to break the news to him that I was going to miss his first basketball game of the season that Saturday. Because of my guilt and his disappointment, I had decided to buy him a new pair of basketball shoes. He really did not need a new pair, but this was my way of handling the situation. He felt let down by my change in plans and could not understand why, after so many hours of helping him practice for this all-important game, I was leaving town instead.

When we arrived home, Kaylon was all decked out in her new riding boots and helmet, prancing around the room pretending she was riding a horse.

"Watch me, Daddy. Watch my horse jump."

She was so excited; her first riding lesson was scheduled for Friday, January 20. I broke the news to her next—that I would miss it also. She was heartbroken as she told me, "It's not fair. You promised you would be there."

I explained that in order for her to have all her nice things, I had to work. That kind of logic didn't mean much to an eight-year-old. We fell into the typical evening routine of dinner and baths, then they went off to bed.

I went to Allen's room to have a talk. He didn't understand why I had to be gone so much of the time. This game was really important to him and he wanted me there—to be proud of him.

"I promise and *I really mean it this time*, Allen, I *will* be home for your next game on Tuesday afternoon," I said, still feeling guilty about disappointing him.

I did not have the heart to go into Kaylon's room and face her again, so I started packing for the trip.

I told Devon that I did not think the time away from the children was worth it. The kids were counting on me this weekend, I said. I mentioned again that maybe I should drop out of the hunting trip to central Alabama with my companions, noting that I really didn't want to go, but Devon encouraged me. "You've already made the commitment," she said.

I told her that I wasn't needed on this trip. My partner was going. These guys weren't going to miss me. I had made up my mind I was staying home for the weekend, when the phone rang. It was one of my business partners making sure I would be on time in the morning. Despite my reservations, I reluctantly agreed to go ahead with the outing. It was important to everyone but my children and wife. Although Devon had encouraged me to go, I knew deep down inside she wanted me to stay. I should have followed my instincts.

It was one more time that I would be putting work and a measure of personal pleasure before my family. Little did I know I would not only miss the entire basketball season, but it would be six months before I would get to see my daughter ride a horse.

Getting to the Woods

A promise is the offspring of the intention and should be nurtured by recollection.—George Herbert

I Didn't Want to Go

January 19th, I was downstairs making coffee, still trying to figure a way to get out of going on the trip. I was tempted to call my partner and tell him I didn't feel well. Then, before I started my coffee, I heard someone knocking on the garage door. My partner had arrived early and was incredibly impatient. I secretly hoped that if I didn't answer the door, perhaps he would leave without me. But finally I gave in to the relentless pounding. I never had my coffee, but the pot was ready for Devon when she awoke. I was too rushed to even go back upstairs to kiss the kids good-bye. Left behind were an empty coffee cup, an unread morning newspaper and my sleeping family.

As I loaded my gear into the truck I thought about my children wanting me to stay to participate in their events, and my understanding wife assuring me that she and the children would be okay. I definitely did not want to go on this hunting trip.

What would I have done differently if I had known that within thirty-six hours my life would change dramatically and that it would be two months before I would return home?

Broken Promise

As I rode in the truck down the highway, I continued to brood. Even a good dad has unfinished business. I had repeatedly promised myself that the kids and Devon would be first in my life. Here I was again yielding to the pressure of business and breaking promises to them. It was the worst of all promises to break. It's also the easiest kind of promise to break. It's the promise you make to yourself. Who is there to hold you accountable to you? As we drove towards Eufala, Alabama, I was overwhelmed with guilt and sorrow. I could not get my family out of my mind.

We checked into the motel and dropped our bags off before heading to the woods for an afternoon hunt. The property where we planned to hunt the next morning was a few miles west of Eufala. After a scouting trip to the woods we returned to our motel to wash up before dinner.

Still feeling guilty, I could not enjoy the woods that afternoon. I did not even bother to load my gun. I left dinner early and walked back to the motel so that I could call home. I even talked with Devon about renting a car and driving back on my own. She, however, urged me to stay, assuring me she and the children would be okay. "A few days in the woods will probably do you some good," she said.

In those days I never took my Bible with me when I traveled. Frustrated and disheartened because of what I felt were my misguided priorities, I sat on my bed and looked for a Gideon's Bible in the nightstand drawer. For some reason I turned to Romans 8:28, *And we know that in all things God works for the good of those who love him, who have been called according to his purpose* (NIV). The verse gave me something to think about. I hoped it was true.

I am a morning person, but 4:30 A.M. still came awfully early. The motel room was chilly, but I was up without any difficulty. It was very cold outside so I put on my long underwear before slipping into my camouflage hunting gear. Breakfast was on everybody's mind, so we went immediately to the local diner before heading to the woods. When we opened the door to the restaurant, the wonderful aroma of bacon, sausage, and southern-style cooking summoned us to the nearest table. The coffee steamed from our cups as we waited for the waitress to bring our order. We made final plans as to where we would hunt and we agreed to meet back at the trucks about noon. This savory breakfast was to be my last real meal for nearly two weeks.

We arrived in the woods well before daylight, and made our way to the prearranged hunting blinds. I, however, remained behind at the truck because I didn't have the heart to go on the hunt. Just after daylight I heard a shot. There is a distinguishing sound when a bullet impacts its target. I figured that one of the fellows in our party "connected."

As it turned out, my location by the truck was pretty good. I spotted more than ten deer as they walked by. Finally, at about 11:00 A.M. a small buck came into range. Normally I would not have shot a small deer, but it was to be my last hunt of the season and I wanted some venison for the freezer. I raised my gun and aimed. *Bang!* My mission was accomplished. As the noon hour approached our group met at the trucks and the "skinning tree."

I gathered up the guns, making sure they were unloaded, wiped them down and put each gun in its appropriate box. Finished, I turned from the trucks and walked the short distance to the skinning tree. One of the men was pulling on a rope as he hoisted the deer up to the level where he could comfortably work on skinning it.

C HAPTE R
3

One Ordinary Tree
and Two Spindly Bucks

Live each day as if it is your last.— Publilius Syrus

As I was walking toward the tree, there was a loud noise like a yardstick breaking over your thigh. The crack pierced the cool air like that of a baseball player hitting a home run ball over the center field. It took only a second for the tree to break from the weight of the deer. There was no time for me to panic, move aside, brace or react in any way. The falling tree struck me across my left shoulder with such a powerful blow that I was crushed and pinned to the ground beneath the mangled mess of a tree and branches.

The skinning tree did not appear weak or frail and the deer we were about to hang in it weren't very big. It was simply a combination of the right amount of torque and angle and the tree simply gave way. No forgotten seat belt or icy road, faulty product or reckless act, it was simply a freak accident. The tree just broke and I was standing in the direction in which it fell. Who would have ever guessed such an accident could occur?

I'm Dying

As I lay underneath the tree, pain and paralysis overwhelmed my body. My arms and legs were immobilized, and breathing was difficult. *I can't breathe. I am dying on this cold Alabama ground.* I did not see any bright lights; I wasn't floating over my body nor was I standing at the River's edge, but I knew I was at life's end. What were Devon and the kids going to do? Who would tell them? Would they cry? How would they remember me? What would my kids tell their children about their dad? They didn't know how much I loved them. I hurriedly left on this trip without saying good-bye. Out of desperation I prayed to God.

Now mind you, it was not one of these fancy prayers in which I acknowledged all the great things God has done. Nor did I include anybody else in my short prayer. It was just me and Him. I prayed for *me*: "God, if it's time to go, I am ready, but I want a second chance to be with my wife and children."

At that very instant I was touched by the Holy Spirit and the pain and paralysis left my chest and arms and breathing became easier. I knew I was going to live and that I was going to walk again. *Walk again?* I was filled with an inner peace and calming spirit.

My lower back ignited in fiery pain, shooting lightning bolts through my legs and down to my feet. The flashes of fire pulsated up and down my motionless legs with angry consistency. I wiggled my fingers, felt the cold ground, then grabbed each side of my chest and ran my hands down beyond my hips as far as my hands could reach. My hands felt my thighs, but my thighs didn't feel back. In fact, there was no sensation below my waist. As I lay on my back with the huge tree on top of me, I looked over and around each of my shoulders. I could see my feet flopped to either side. I tried to raise my legs and move my feet. No response. I knew I was paralyzed from the waist down. I had no movement and the only sensation was the searing jolts of pain running through my legs and feet.

My companions gathered at my head and discussed pulling me out from under the tree. I objected, telling them I had broken my back and was paralyzed from the waist down. They continued to debate. I really hadn't broken my back, they guessed. Maybe it was just a hip or leg or something. "No my back is broken! I know it!" I looked up at my companions and said, "Two of you have cell phones. You better call an ambulance."

A feeling of dread started to overtake me. I was scared! I don't know what goes through the mind of someone else in a situation like this, but I started thinking about my immediate limitations. While two of my companions were trying to call for help I asked the one who remained a question. Had I wet my pants? The only thing I thought I knew about paralyzed people was that they have no bladder control. He answered no, and I had a sense of relief—for a second. Then my thoughts flashed to me sitting on the beach digging my toes into the sand and riding a bike. I would never walk again or pick up and hold my children or enjoy the basketball games and horseback riding lessons that we had planned together.

My feeling of dread was overcome by fear and doubt. The father of one of my companions had broken his back some fifty years earlier. I knew I could draw strength from this man and asked him if he thought I was going to be okay. I could see the alarm in his eyes. Maybe it reflected what he saw in mine. I wanted something to drink and he brought me a stale soda.

Where was the ambulance? They were having trouble getting a signal on the cell phones! "Walk around, drive out to the hard road, do something!" I demanded. "Get someone on the phone, please." I wanted my wife and kids. I just wanted to get away from here.

Finally, they told me they were able to get through to 911 and help was on the way.

But where was the ambulance?

"One of you go out to the hard road and wait for it. They will not know which dirt road to take up here to where we are," I said. I had to insist that someone go out to the hard road and watch for it. Finally, I heard a siren off in the distance. Were they coming for me? All I wanted to do was get away. *Maybe this would all just vanish and I will awaken from my nightmare.*

The siren was getting louder and I knew it was my ride. The Holy Spirit had gotten ahold of me again and I felt calm and confident once more. I wasn't quite ready to entertain guests, but I knew I was going to live.

Word Travels Fast in the Back Woods

Another hunter appeared. He talked with my companions, but kept his distance. I was glad because I felt strangely ashamed to be lying here on the ground underneath this tree. It was humiliating to be so helpless. I saw a wildlife officer and then someone from the forestry service arrive. I hadn't done anything wrong. Why were they here? They never spoke directly to me. As I tried to look at those gathering around, I could feel the grinding and crunching of broken bones in my back when I moved slightly or even breathed.

The ambulance siren stopped and before long I heard the sound of its engine making its way through the woods. *Why did this have to be me? I don't cheat on my wife. I don't hit the kids. I work in earnest to see that others are treated fairly. When I am in town, I go to church nearly every Sunday.*

I couldn't see the ambulance, but I could smell the exhaust fumes as it parked a few feet behind my head. Out of the vehicle stepped a man and a woman. *The man was driving and that explained why it took so long,* I laughed to myself. *No doubt, he had directions but probably didn't follow them. It's a guy thing.* The woman knelt on the ground peering at me through the tangled mess of a tree and told me her name was Alice. She asked me my name, as if it should matter. If I said Al, would she stand back up explaining that they were looking for a Bob who was also pinned under a tree and someone else would be by for me later? Her face was reassuring and her demeanor was calming. She was a real quizzer, however. She wanted to know more than just my name. What was the time of day? What's the day of the week? What's the date? I stopped her right there and said I didn't know the date and didn't really care. I know now she was merely assessing my state of mind, and whether or not I was in shock. At the time I had had enough.

She began to perform the standard emergency routine of administering oxygen, placing a neck brace and started an IV. Then she had to go about the arduous task of extracting me from underneath the fallen tree. The danger was twofold. The first problem was: The tree was resting twelve to fourteen inches over my chest. A miscalculation would cause the tree to fall at any second. Next, I had to be moved without further complicating my injuries. Alice told me not to panic, but they were going to place a sheet over my body and head. Cover me like a corpse! Yes, it did bother me! Was I dead or dying? I had just had a near-death experience and did not want anyone covering me with a sheet.

I objected, but Alice was in charge. The sheet, she explained, was to protect me from the chain saw debris. Alice directed the men who took positions around the tree to secure it as another began cutting away. I could smell the wood heat and burn as the saw blades ripped through limbs and branches. As the cutter got closer to my body, the hot air produced by the chain saw hissed in my face and wood chips pelted the sheet. Now for the hard part. Alice then instructed several of those who gathered on how to properly roll me over so she could slip a backboard underneath me.

I Was Not Prepared for What Was about to Happen

Alice got down on her hands and knees again and told me this was going to really hurt, but they had to get me onto a backboard. She offered me a stick, a tongue depressor or something to bite down on while they rolled me over, but I declined. Alice said on the count of three I would be rolled over. Three sets of hands securely grabbed me on my left side. *One, two . . .* and the men rolled me over to the right. I don't remember hearing the third count, but to this day, and until the day I die, I will remember my scream of pain as it echoed through the woods. I have no doubt it impacted those hovering over me. The body has a built-in safety device and it will shut down when it can't take any more. I passed out.

I don't know how long I remained on the ground or how long I was unconscious, but I came to as they passed me through the rear doors of the ambulance. Two painful thuds and whacks hit my back-side as the wheel and leg system of the stretcher locked into place. I looked around inside the ambulance and wondered if I would be able to hear the siren from the inside. That was something I have always wanted to know and now I was going to find out firsthand.

My attention was drawn immediately back to the unbearable pain. I asked Alice if she could give me something for it. Her response blew me away. She told me her ambulance did not carry pain medication. She instead asked me if I wanted her to pray for me. I was at a point in my life that prayer sounded pretty good. She prayed, "God give this young man peace of mind and the doctors the knowledge to do what is necessary to help him." I think she really said man, but I threw in the "young" part myself. Not a fancy prayer, but it worked. Her prayer reminded me that I had already encountered God once that morning and I knew I was going to be all right.

God does not always answer prayers the way you expect Him to. I was still in pain, but was reassured and calm.

Yes, I could hear the siren and could feel every horrid bump. The driver had difficulty getting out of the woods. Each lurch sent an angry message to every broken bone in my back. The pain was overwhelming as I pleaded for him to slow down. Alice assured me that the ride would be easier once we were out on the paved road. I think the local highway department had marked all the potholes in the road so the ambulance driver could find them. If the bumps were not enough, I was sure that he was taking the turns extra hard just to break up the monotony of the regular road hazards. Eventually, the drive became blurred as we raced to the small hospital in Eufala.

Small Town Emergency Room

Of all the things you wear., your expression is the most important.
— Janet Lane

My awareness peaked as I was unloaded from the ambulance and taken into the emergency room. Eufala doesn't sound like a town that would have a very big hospital and it didn't. It certainly was not like the one you see on the television series "ER," but I was glad to be there.

I was wheeled into a small room crowded with emergency personnel and got the same set of questions that Alice had just asked me. I told them I had taken that test already. The medical staff prepared me for X rays by cutting away my favorite camouflage pants and long underwear. As one of the attendants started unlacing my shoes, I said, "Just cut them off. I won't need them anymore."

The man taking off my boots paused a moment and sternly said, "You are not going to talk like that with us. Okay?"

"Sure," I replied.

I still have those hunting boots, but I never got my pants and long underwear back. I figured the staff thought I would get mad or something.

Then I started wondering, where was Alice? I had bonded with her and I wanted her at my side. They took the X rays and someone told me the doctor would be in right away. I was surrounded by emergency medical staff, but I only remember one face in the examination room. It was that of a young woman. She had alarm and worry written all over her face. I felt lost. Then, in came the doctor and he told me what I already had figured out. I had broken several vertebrae and I was paralyzed from the waist down. *Oh really! Tell me something I don't already know.* What about the pain? He told me they were going to give me morphine and the steroid methylprednisolone. Looking back, the best medication I received that day was that steroid, which helped reduce the swelling around my spinal cord and inhibited further injury. The doctor said I needed to be transported to a larger medical facility for emergency surgery and treatment. By now I knew I was not going to make it home for the weekend.

I was prepared for the hour-long ambulance ride to Dothan's Southeast Regional Medical Center. The room cleared of all the medical staff except for one fellow who told me he was going to insert a Foley catheter. I was already lying there in the bare-naked truth. Why did the other staff members decide to allow me privacy now? I told him, pointing to the IV in my arm, that I already had one of those. They all knew what a Foley catheter was. I didn't.

My first medical lesson was about to begin. I had my privacy and the Foley catheter. I watched the procedure, as the young man said, "Don't worry, this will not bother you."

Yeah, you got that right. I was pumped full of morphine and had no sensation from the waist down. What did he expect!

Taking Charge

By now the effects of the morphine were consuming me. I overheard the EMTs talking with one another and realized that another ambulance crew was taking me to Dothan. This was going to be the first of many take-charge steps along this rocky medical road. I insisted—no demanded—that Alice had to go with me. She was my safety net. I didn't care if these were different ambulance companies or different teams or whatever. I didn't think about Alice needing to go home to her family that evening. All I knew was that Alice got me this far and I wanted her on that ambulance for the ride to Dothan. She made the trip, but it was probably not necessary after all as I slipped off into the twilight and slumber of the pain medication. She told me later that occasionally I would awaken and ask, "What happened? Where am I?" Mostly, I simply succumbed to a sleepy and restless storm in my head.

CHAPTER 5

Dothan after Hours

Until you make your peace with who you are, you'll never be content with what you are.—Doris Mortman

I don't recall being unloaded from the ambulance, but I found myself in another emergency room. There were more X rays and a trip through a donut-looking contraption—the MRI, as I later learned. (Now I have so much hardware in my back that I can't go through this procedure anymore.) The ceiling lights blurred above my head as I was wheeled from one exam room to another. I was pretty much out of it by then. My only recollection of the first hour or so at the hospital in Dothan was when my gurney pilots would hit every door threshold with a painful jar. *Please, take it easy going over the bumps.* The first batch of morphine was wearing off.

Where is Devon, I wondered? I was told that my wife could not be located. I wanted to talk with her. I wanted to be reassured and to reassure her that everything was going to be okay.

After enduring the passage through the MRI not once, but twice, I was exhausted. The technician told me he wanted to make sure the surgeon had every picture he needed. I thought the technician was actually asleep at the wheel during the first time through the machine. Waiting for the surgeon to arrive was pure torture. The morphine was continuing to wear off and I was in pain. I still wanted to call home. I was no longer thinking about Alice. I wanted my wife—the woman I had so many times deserted while I had gone away on business or hunting trips.

My stretcher was rolled out to a hallway while we waited for the surgeon to arrive. I saw a phone nearby on the wall. Just my luck it had a short cord, but I managed to get a call through to Devon.

"Where have you been?" I asked. Oh yes, she and Kaylon spent the afternoon at her first riding lesson. I had forgotten about the lesson. I should have been there. I don't recall what we talked about, but I am sure I was pleasant and did not tell her how upset I had been when I could not reach her earlier in the day from Eufala.

The doctor, a neurosurgeon, reviewed the films and finally met with me. He was easy to talk with and I liked him. He told me I had two choices: I could lie immobile in bed for six months and wait for the broken vertebrae to heal. *Not a good plan, I wanted to get home by the first of the week.* Or, he could operate on me the next day, repairing and fusing the broken vertebrae. I wanted to be aggressive, and said, "Let's operate." I was still hoping that I could make it home by the end of the following week. I had not realized the extent of my injuries.

He told me he would set surgery for noon the next day. "Doctor, I told you I wanted to be aggressive. What's wrong with first thing in the morning?"

It seems he had a prior engagement on the basketball court with a city basketball team. I was aggravated, but wasn't in a position to argue with him. Before he left he said, "I will see to it that you rest comfortably tonight."

More morphine? Oh goody, knock me out. He asked if there was anything else he could do for me and I asked him to remember me in his prayers. I did not want to put him on the spot by asking him to pray for me—just a simple "remember me." His response was shocking, "I don't pray."

As he left I had a sinking feeling. Did God really touch me in the woods? Did I not need any more prayers? Feelings of uncertainty grabbed my soul, tears filled my eyes and the morphine took care of the rest.

CHAPTER 6

Family on Notice

When written in Chinese, the word "crisis" is composed of two characters—one represents danger and the other represents opportunity.

The First Surgery

I have often wondered what it would be like to be on the receiving end of tragic news, but never thought I would be the one the message was about. Who would have ever guessed that a tree would give way, break and aim right toward me before I could get out of its way?

The surgeon called Devon and discussed the seriousness of my injury and the uncertainty of my future. I don't know how I would have reacted if I had been on the receiving end of such a call. I have heard several accounts of the reports back home. Friends could not believe it. I had the reputation of being an overly cautious and careful hunter. Hurt in a hunting accident? Not Al! Accounts ranged from "he was not expected to live," to "make funeral arrangements." Other rumors said that I had been shot, fell out of a tree, hurt my back and would need a little back surgery. A "little surgery" was right. Devon set about making plans to fly to Dothan early the next morning before the surgery began. I wondered if she would have time to drop by and watch my surgeon playing basketball on the city league. As far as I was concerned his rear end better be in bed getting some rest. Devon made arrangements for a member of my family to take care of Allen and Kaylon in our home. However, plans changed at the last minute and the kids ended up coming to Dothan. Looking back, I don't know if that was the right decision, but they survived with flying colors.

I'm not sure how long my hunting companions remained. It was an afternoon roller-coaster ride for everyone. However, two lifelong pals, Freddy and Tommy, swung into action. They chartered an airplane and arrived at the hospital about the same time Devon did. I needed my wife and my two buddies with me. Freddy, Tommy and I had been through many good times together. They represented everything positive in my past—the memories, the boyhood dreams, the college camaraderie. As in the good times, they would be by my side, and with Devon, as I faced the most serious six hours so far in my life.

My wife represented the present and future. We had been married for fifteen years at the time of the accident. When I proposed to her on the shores of New Smyrna Beach one evening, she did not accept at first, but asked me why I wanted to marry her. We had dated for nearly two years and I thought we were heading in the same direction with our lives. I told her I wanted someone strong enough to carry on in the event something happened to me. Now calamity happened and it was up to her to do just that. It would take time for me to learn exactly what that would mean for both of us.

It was mid-morning Saturday and I was in intensive care waiting for surgery when they all arrived. Because of all the medication, I recall seeing only silhouettes of people, but heard their voices quite clearly. As they saw me off to the operating room, I made some kind of joke with Tommy about a subpoena. I recall nothing else. Devon and I did not have any meaningful conversation.

Surgery

I briefly came to as the medical staff rolled me over on my stomach and placed my face in a donut-like device to keep me immobile for the scheduled six hours of back surgery. I guess my basketball-playing doctor showed up. The surgery started just after noon with an incision beginning just below my shoulder blades, cutting down in a southward direction until the surgeon couldn't cut anymore. Okay, you can figure where he stopped. Just above my waist, on the left side, he made a diagonal incision a little over four inches long. This one was necessary in order to harvest bone from my pelvis to use as bone-graft material. The body does not know the difference between a broken bone and a "harvest site" and to this day I have as much pain there as I do where bones were actually broken bones. The surgeon performed a laminectomy and vertebrectomy on several of the broken vertebrae. He then stabilized his handiwork with bone from my hip, two Herrington rods and Wisconsin wiring. He described the work as so stable that he could literally lift me off the table by the rods.

While I was in surgery Devon was inspired to make a prophetic statement. She optimistically proclaimed, "Al will walk again. He will backpack and hunt and fish just like he has done in the past." This assertion was met with scorn and disapproval by some members of my family, who had arrived and were waiting with her. They were ready to give up on me. But not my wife, the one who asked why I wanted to marry her. She left the room and took a walk to the doors leading to the operating room. We soon learned that their scornful reaction to her optimism was the first sign that other troubles were to follow with the family.

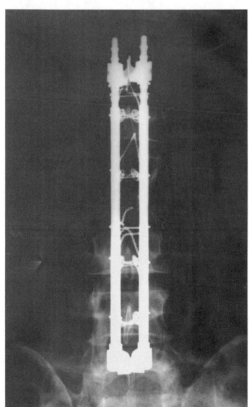

The X ray shows the Herrington rods.

Intensive Care

Close your eyes as tightly as you can and look into a bright light. That's what my vision of intensive care was like. I was placed on a Roto bed, strapped in so I couldn't fall out. This medieval contraption rotates from side to side twenty-four hours a day to prevent blood clots from forming after surgery. It is most unsettling because some of the teeth on the gears that made the bed rotate, were missing. As a result, it would hang at about a forty-five-degree angle and jerk until it met the next tooth.

A television set was suspended from the wall. Rose Kennedy died while I was in intensive care. I thought it was a dream, until some months later when I saw an old magazine article. Someone in the room next to me died of a gunshot wound. Family members cried, as the medical staff tried to comfort them. I have always worried and wondered what happened to that family.

All I wanted to do was sleep and to get through this bad dream. At one point I told Devon I did not want to be touched unless I was spoken to. So she made two signs, one at the head of my bed and one at the foot, which read: PLEASE SPEAK BEFORE TOUCHING ME.

My body was swollen almost beyond recognition from all the methylprednisolone I was given. The doctor ordered a pair of high-top tennis shoes for me to wear while I was in intensive care. This was to help prevent foot drop. I normally wear a size ten, but my feet were so swollen that they would not fit into the shoes.

As I improved, I was transferred to the progressive care unit on January 25, and I began the task of reclaiming my life. It now started to sink in that I was in pretty bad shape, and it would be a long time before I could go home. During my first morning in progressive care,

I was greeted by two young and enthusiastic therapists, Dan and Laurie, who outlined my therapy routine. They started by having me lift a couple of three-pound weights to build up the strength in my arms. I couldn't do it. My body was so ravaged by my injury and postoperative trauma that even these small weights were too much to handle. So instead, I tried lifting a small can of peas. As I recognized my limitations, I started seeing the stress this was causing my family. My sense of accomplishment and means of evaluating things changed. I was quickly learning that there were no good or bad days, just good or bad moments.

We discussed alternative rehabilitation centers, and their amenities, and my future therapy program, as if I were going to a resort or health spa. The Shepherd Spinal Center, now known as the Shepherd Center, sent a representative to meet and evaluate me. I was nervous— fearful a rejection would indicate a poor prognosis. I decided to go to Shepherd if they would have me. Before I could be released anywhere, I would need to pass the standing table test , another medieval device. It was a requirement of the hospital in Dothan. No big deal, strap me to a table and stand me upright. This would prove to be much harder than I ever expected.

Moving On Up

Life isn't a matter of milestones, but moments.—Rose Kennedy

I improved in progressive care and was moved to a regular room on January 29th. As I settled into my bed, I looked at the ceiling, and saw it was covered with dried spitballs. Hmmm, this was just too much of an opportunity for me to pass on. I knew I had to add to the collection.

I decided that during my first time alone, I would add to the messy arrangement. I prepared my wet payload and to my astonishment, I was too weak to blow through the straw. The nurse had told me to call if I needed anything, but I don't think this task applied. So to the housekeeping staff at the hospital in Dothan, it wasn't me.

I started worrying about my future and my past. I did not want sleeping pills and at night I fought sleep. Was I being punished by God for some transgression?

All I wanted to do was talk, and the decision was made to hire a night attendant to listen to me. Looking back on it, having some stranger listen to me all night does not make much sense, but it allowed Devon to get some rest.

I learned that this standing table business was really serious. The device looked more like a bed than a table. Dan and Laurie would transfer me from my hospital bed and then strap me onto the table so I could not fall or slide off.

After I was securely strapped to the table, one of them would turn a crank, which would slowly raise the table and patient a few vertical degrees at first. As my tolerance increased, the objective was 90 degrees without passing out. It is hard to look back and imagine I could only manage a few vertical degrees before my blood pressure brought me to the point of passing out.

It was a frustrating, painful and an exhausting beginning on my long road to recovery. Even though the standing table therapy was going poorly, the doctor said it was time for me to begin sitting upright and he ordered a reclining chair for my room. Besides, he thought it would help me build my tolerance for being upright at the standing table. I peered over the side of the bed and looked down at the chair, which seemed a Grand Canyon away and wondered how I ever was going to get down there. Since surgery I had been fearful that I would be dropped during a "transfer" and would have to endure even more surgery. A transfer is a term commonly used to describe moving a paralyzed body from one point to another. Usually the transfer involves a short distance from a wheelchair to a bed or front seat of a car. In my case, the transfer would be from my hospital bed to a nearby reclining chair.

Never Trust a Woman with a Chewing-Gum Tooth.

I was told the next morning that this was the day I would be transferred from my bed to the recliner. Since I was still too weak to attempt a move on my own, this first transfer was going to be accomplished with the help of two attendants. They had the distinguished looks of backwoods country sharecroppers. As the first attendant walked through the door she announced, "Were a harr to git ye up in that thar char." These two helpers were skinny as a rail and the woman was missing a front tooth. I objected to them moving me as I feared they were not strong enough and would surely drop me. I should have trusted my instinct, but gave in to their insistence. This toothless granny said, "Don't wary, honey, I have a done dis a hundered time." She and her younger helper picked me up with one quick swing and hurled me from the bed to recliner. What I know now is the experience she referred to involved slinging sacks of potatoes from mule wagon to a loading dock.

After dropping me in the recliner she replaced the missing front tooth with chewing gum and was grinning ear to ear. She said, "See thar, I tol ye I coulda do it."

I don't know if Granny had anything to do with it, but within a short time my strength began to return and I started to feed myself.

Subtle Reminder

It didn't matter the time of day or night, many people were very interested in the uniqueness of my accident and they would come in just to hear me tell the story. Sometimes they were from administration or maybe they were medical staffers donning latex gloves as they tended to my needs. Because of all the curiosity and questions I felt like a lab specimen.

If you have ever spent any time in the hospital you know that no one knocks on the door when they enter your room. Maybe visitors will make a timid announcement as they enter, but they don't knock either. One weekend night well after 10:00 P.M., there *was* a knock at the door. This is unusual for anyone, especially a weekend staffer—generally the least desirable of the nursing team.

Well, the staffer kept knocking—like a paralyzed guy could hop up out of bed and open the door for guests.

"Come in," I said. In walked a woman who asked, "Do you know who I am?"

"Yes, you're Alice," I responded. My companion in the ambulance had volunteered to make a return trip to Dothan on another case so she could stop and visit me. She told me I was such an inspiration that she had to come back to meet me under better circumstances. She said she had never seen a person with a catastrophic injury like mine who was at peace.

Admittedly, the circumstances of my accident had been unusual and I was growing tired of repeating them to new staff. But this was not a staffer who was calling on me tonight. I had told others about the tree falling on me, but Alice was the first person I felt comfortable telling about my encounter with God, perhaps because she had talked of God during the ambulance ride. I told her, "He answered my prayer as I lay on the ground."

Our visit was brief and Alice soon returned to Eufala. I had been having some doubts about my encounter with God the day I was hurt. This was His first reminder, a reassuring sign, that it really happened. I knew then and there that I had to get things straight in my life if I was to call on God again for help. When you seek His help, God doesn't qualify you, like a loan officer scrutinizes a loan applicant, but I knew inside that I had unresolved business.

The next evening I placed a call to my father in Orlando. We had not spoken since February 1986, at his mother's funeral. My parents were divorced when I was thirteen, and since I was fifteen he and I had probably not had more than two meaningful conversations. Maybe my motive was selfish and self-centered, but I needed to set things straight between us. I called him to bury the hatchet. I don't recall any details of our conversation, but I did not ask forgiveness or give forgiveness. I just hoped it was implied with my call. My father offered to come, to take care of my children—to do whatever he could. I could hear earnest despair in his voice. I could not accept his offer because of the tension with other family members, but I promised I would call him again. All I was after was personal peace of mind so I could selfishly work on my recovery. I felt my mission had been accomplished for the time being.

The Day

By now the physical therapists and I had a routine. Dan and Laurie would come once in the morning and again in the afternoon to strap me onto the standing table. The Shepherd Spinal Center had accepted me, but if I were ever to leave this place I needed to get upright for several moments without passing out. I was strong enough and my blood pressure maintained sufficient levels to keep me from getting light-headed, but the pain was intolerable. We kept working. The standing table test was also necessary to see if the fusion and instrumentation would hold up under the stress of my body weight in an upright position.

Finally, the day came when I passed the test. Dan and Laurie were excited by my success and wasted no time calling my surgeon and the radiology department right from my room. Everything now hinged on what the next set of X rays showed. We needed to see if the surgeon's handiwork held together. I was whisked off to radiology. Everyone on my wing seemed eager to see and hear the results. In fact, the hospital staff stopped what they were doing to applaud as I passed them by on my way to radiology. I felt exhilarated, like a prize fighter being ushered to the ring for the championship fight. I entered my ring . . . and won the fight.

The film revealed everything held together and then the celebration began. Tears flowed as we all knew I could now leave this place and get into a rehabilitation program.

Back in my room depression and fear hit me like a freight train. This was the first time since my injury that I experienced a big letdown and bottomed out. What was going to happen next? How was I going to get along when I got home? I did not know where to turn. I would pray as I fell asleep. I wanted a miracle. I wanted to turn back time and make this all go away.

The Flight

My flight to Atlanta by air ambulance was scheduled for the next day. My mother, who had been at the hospital these first few weeks, was not handling my injury very well and she left for Atlanta to meet me on the receiving end. Looking back, she would have been better off to have gone home to rest and collect herself. Devon and I had dinner together in the room that night. I was "down" and exhausted from the last several days of therapy. Also worn out, Devon did her best to revive me from my deep decline. I recalled Vince Lombardi telling his players, "Fatigue makes cowards of us all." That was it, I was just tired. Thanks, coach! But I could not sleep.

Since my accident I had been reduced to a pile of human rubble, but the day I was scheduled to leave the hospital, I scored another victory. I had gained enough strength to shave myself and I lay in bed waiting, cleanly shaven for Devon's arrival. She was gathering up my meager hospital belongings for the flight. I felt great, ready to take on the world. Now, where was that airplane?

Nothing is easy. The departure time was moved from 11:00 A.M. to noon and finally 2:00 P.M. I was wondering if I was going to get to leave that day. Had something happened and they were not telling me? I was ready to get on with the process and did not want any more delays. I knew I was going to be at Shepherd for a while—six to eight weeks. I wanted to get started with its program as quickly as possible.

Overall, my stay at the Southeast Regional Hospital was wonderful. I made a few nurses uneasy, however, when they saw me making notes in a diary. I wanted the names of all the people who had helped me. But word spread quickly that I was asking for names and writing them down. One young nurse, whose name badge was always turned over, refused to give me hers. She told me they all knew I was planning a lawsuit and she did not want to be a part of it. The truth of the matter was that I intended to write thank-you notes to those who helped me. No one received a summons to appear in court, but they all received a personal note from me. It is a shame that society has become so litigious that even the simplest of human gestures can be misconstrued.

The EMTs finally arrived to take me for the short ride to the airport. I checked to see if I had a shadow on my face after this delay and would need to shave again. Devon followed the ambulance to the airport. From one checkpoint to another, each team signed me over to the other as if this were some kind of a prisoner exchange. Each team made sure I was not damaged on its watch. As we waited on the tarmac, I told the attendants to lower the stretcher so I could feel the ground. Though it was only cold concrete, this was my first contact with the outside world since a major injury twelve days earlier. The air was crisp and smelled clean. The high blue sky caused me to squint as I looked around the airport. My system had become adjusted to the stale and sterile atmosphere of the hospital environment. I was sneezing, but it was refreshing to be outside once again.

I looked across the tarmac at the air ambulance, a King Air. I used to fly on King Airs during my early twenties when I was a political aide in Tallahassee. This brought back many wonderful memories, but I also was wondering how these guys were going to get me through the door. I recalled that a few days earlier, the woman with the chewing-gum tooth said, "Trust me." I made sure these guys knew I was uneasy about squeezing into the plane. I did not want to be dropped again forcing a return to the Dothan hospital.

These fellows had all their teeth and I made it on the plane without incident. My stretcher was secured in its place and we prepared for takeoff. I felt like I was flying first class as the flight attendant/ nurse offered me something to drink before departure. Coca-Cola. I wanted a Coke and drank several during the hour-long flight to Atlanta. After all my apprehension and the delays, I ended up having a wonderful time with the flight crew.

When we arrived in Atlanta, the crew signed me over to the ground crew. Nothing was damaged so we headed to Shepherd by ambulance. I think these Atlanta EMTs were on loan from animal control. They were not very friendly and were uncommunicative. I felt like just another stray dog being hauled off to the pound where he would be adopted and neutered or put to sleep. Why talk to the cargo headed for such a destination? Ground crew aside, the flight to Atlanta helped me remember who I was. It took me back to the days of political campaigns and puddle-hopping. I felt at home and in control, if only in my imagination.

Admission to Shepherd

Real difficulties can be overcome. It is only the imaginary ones
that are unconquerable.—Theodore Vail

I was getting good at counting the ceiling tiles and fluorescent lights overhead as I was wheeled back and forth through the corridors of the hospital. Today, though, as I entered the reception area of Shepherd, I wasn't counting tiles and lights. I looked around, trying to catch someone's eye for a reassuring glance, signaling to me everything was okay—yeah, I know about your talk with God and that you are going to walk again. That did not happen. I felt small and conspicuously insignificant as I was wheeled into a room for more X rays and admission processing. I tried to joke my way through the ordeal, but I was just plain uneasy. I wanted to go home and forget any of this happened to me.

Swimming Pools and Movie Stars

There were two reasons I picked Shepherd. The first was because of the indoor swimming pool, and the second, each bed had a television. This was important because all my life, when I was away from home, I slept with the television turned on. None of us talked much about the actual details of therapy, just a few of the amenities, as we truly had no concept of what therapy was going to be like. I was prone to involuntaries (unexpected bowel movements) and made it to the pool only once. And I was soon to learn that they would make me turn off the television when I needed it most—as a late night diversion. *What have I gotten myself into?* I thought. *Could this place possibly offer any other services?*

I was officially admitted and received a nice new blue wristband. An attendant then wheeled my stretcher, to my room where I met my roommates. Whoa, they were not what I expected! How could I be in a place like this? I am not in this kind of shape. Or, was I? We were four to a room and our beds were separated by curtains. Across from me was Steve, a striking young African-American and a quadriplegic. It seemed that Steve had been wrestling with his cousin in their living room and his cousin did a power drive using Steve as the driving instrument. It was a move they had probably seen on television, but nobody got hurt on TV. I never met his cousin, but he had to have been huge, because Steve was an imposing figure himself. He was visited often by friends who would bring him cigarettes and he spent a good part of his day propelling himself outside for a smoke.

In the bed next to me was Tuyen, a Vietnamese immigrant. He had broken his neck in a car accident. Tuyen's injury level was higher than Steve's. Tuyen was older and struggling for and with life. I often think of Tuyen and how his life has been since he left Shepherd. He served his country as an officer in the war, then came to the United States and this happened. It was very sad.

Duffy was in the bed across from Tuyen. He was walking, and I wanted to get to know this guy. Unfortunately, he was released before I learned his secrets of walking. Later I was told he had been in a minor traffic accident and was thrown around in the vehicle. He wasn't wearing a seat belt. He had never really lost his mobility. He was not the inspiration I was looking for, nevertheless he was walking. I was paralyzed from the waist down with a promise from God.

During my first evening at Shepherd, I was visited by a young doctor who identified himself as the person who would be in charge of my case. He said he had reviewed my charts and asked me if I had any questions.

"Yeah, how long will it be before I am able to walk?"

He reminded me he was familiar with my case and said that it wouldn't happen. My injuries were severe. I would not walk. I told him about my prayer and that promise from God.

"Well, okay, you might be able to stand propped up and using two full metal leg braces," he said, saying that I would be confined to such activity in my home. Actually, he used the word "housebound." I did not like the idea that I was only going to be able to roll up to my kitchen window in my wheelchair, and maybe, just maybe, by pulling up to the sink and locking two full leg braces into place look out at the world. There was a chance your insurance company will provide you with a standing table, he said.

No way, I thought, as I remembered my previous experience with that unpleasant contraption. Nope, this was not my story line.

He told me that his job and the job of the staff was to train me to become independent enough to care for myself. I told him I was going to walk again and that my faith in God would pull me through. All I got from him was a blank stare. He continued to say that he was very confident that the staff would help me progress and that I would be independent. Needless to say I did not care for the guy and made it clear I did not want to see him again.

Then, I did what any grown man would do in a situation like this. My eyes welled up with tears and I wept. I was looking at the ceiling, searching for comfort. The doctor left me feeling like the victim of a hit-and-run, when in walked Bob, my nurse. He was great. He turned a chair around backwards and sat down, resting his arms on the chair back. We had an earnest, heart-to-heart talk about my well-being and the many ways I was going to benefit from the rehabilitation program.

"Am I going to walk again? I *am* going to walk again! I know it, because God told me so," I told him.

Bob was somewhat comforting, but he, too, had been briefed by the doctor. I told Bob I wanted to speak with a chaplain. He told me he would get him, but soon returned telling me the chaplain would be gone for several days. I asked him if there was someone on staff who would come and pray with me. He left and later returned, telling me there was no one who could do that. I felt I had been deserted by God and wondered again if He really had come to me in the woods. I felt I was justified in my doubts. Look where I was. What happened to all that confidence I had while flying on that King Air?

I felt so alone. Devon was on her way by car.

I had come to the rehabilitation center with high hopes and in good spirits. Yet, here it was my first night and my hopes and spirits were not just broken, they were splattered about on the floor. My plans and dreams were crushed. The brave me could not rise to the surface. Drowning in disbelief, I knew I was now going to learn what it was like to have to dig deep and fight hard. I fell asleep praying to God for peace and strength. Tomorrow had to be better.

A Bright New Day

Boarding schools, summer camps and military boot camps have reveille to awaken the slumbering masses and bring the assemblage to order. I found that spinal centers have their own way of waking you. I was awakened before daylight by two imposing figures who identified themselves only as urologists!

For all I knew they were a couple of curious aliens. They pulled back my bedsheets, lifted up my hospital gown, pausing just a moment to stare at my privates and vanished through the door before I could say, "Welcome to earth. Do you come in peace? Hey, is this some kind of survey or contest?"

I wanted to know! My attention turned to a discussion I overheard in my room about bowel and bladder programs. I knew that wasn't for me. I had only suffered a broken back. My plumbing was working just fine. My thoughts wandered back to the recent visit of the urologists, whom I later nicknamed Dr. Granite and Dr. Ice to match their personalities.

Well, who's next? I wondered. *Will anyone else stop by this morning? How do you get some food around this place?* I met the "reassuring" doctor last night and then this morning Drs. Granite and Ice. Then came another visitor, a member of the hospital staff. Her name was Margaret. She was a kind-looking woman, but she had a merciless mission. She told me she was here to remove my Foley catheter— the one I received in the emergency room in Eufala. It was probably changed along the way, perhaps during surgery, but I didn't recall it. I was happy to get rid of it so that I could start relieving myself the old "regular" way—not through a flexible straw attached to a nagging drainage bag. This was my first introduction into the world of paraplegics and quadriplegics.

Margaret and the Foley

Back in Dothan my surgeon told me I had lost control of everything below my waist including motor and sensory functions. I had not eaten much food for the last two weeks and I did not give the matter of elimination any thought. Bladder control had not crossed my mind ever since I had a Foley catheter. While Margaret was removing the tubing, she told me that someone named Rick would be in later to explain my bowel and bladder program. Oh, gosh. At the time of the accident I asked one of my hunting partners if I had wet my pants. Now I knew that was not possible because my bladder had been shut down in the "off" position. I was about to learn all about intermittent catheterization, or "I.C." in the vernacular of those of us in the "wheel world." I was in a state of shock when I learned that I was going to have to do this every four to six hours for the rest of my life. It might be six hours if I learned how to limit my fluid intake. I was accustomed to drinking a quart of water every morning. Forget talking about quarts or even pints. These guys were speaking in terms of intake and output as cc this and cc that. They meant business. My intake placed me on the four-hour schedule. I was beyond the point of being embarrassed by anything. The reality was very hard to accept and most humbling, but not nearly as humbling as when I asked Margaret if I was going to have to do something special for the other ahh . . . well, you know. Earlier in the morning I heard staff talking about the bowel program with another one of the patients in my room. She said, "That's not my job. You need to see Rick or Bob about that."

Margaret left, and like clockwork in walked, Rick, my nurse's aide, to give me my first lesson in the methods of the I.C. If given a choice, many SCI (spinal cord injury) patients will say they will choose the return of their bowel and bladder function over walking. Everything from diet to travel and work routines must be planned ahead. I have learned from experience that it is not difficult to establish a routine to fit a busy schedule. You simply plan your activities in advance.

The next visits that morning would be from my physical and occupational therapists and, yes, we patients all got to see the shrink. The therapists' job was to assess me for a rehabilitation program. They were glad that I had something to work with. I was exhilarated until I learned that they meant my upper body. I was going to need my arms and shoulders for transfer and pushing my wheelchair. My occupational therapists were going to teach me how to do everything from getting dressed to bathing, cooking and other household chores. I wanted no part of her or her training. I never went around my house without a shirt on, and now I was about to let some stranger teach me how to dress and bathe. The therapists asked my family to purchase several pairs of sweat pants because they would be easier for me to put on and would also keep me warm. I have always been a bit of a nonconformist, so when I had the opportunity I cut the legs off all my new pants. I wanted to be able to see my legs, even if they did not work. Every chance I had, I would visualize my legs moving.

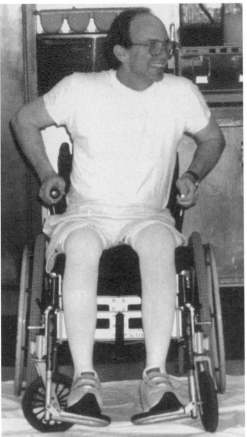

March 8, 1995 at Shepherd Spinal Center. I was wearing my "cut-offs" and sporting the thigh-high T.E.D.s.

When your legs and hips don't work properly, there is a definite routine you must go through in getting dressed. First, you need to get dressed while lying down, which was definitely difficult in the beginning. I was kind of glad I had cut the legs off my pants—there was less fabric to deal with. Worst of all about getting dressed were the thigh-high T.E.D. (anti-embolism) stockings I had to wear. They were necessary to assist in circulation and to keep blood clots from forming in my legs. I never did get the knack of putting them on. Thank goodness I only have to wear the knee-highs now.

A Real Bath at Last

During my second night at Shepherd I took a real shower. It had been nearly two weeks since my injury and I hadn't had a real bath. I really think they wanted to clean me up before I met the shrink the next morning. I had no idea what was in store for me during the shower, but I would be in the capable hands of my dedicated attendant, Rick.

However, it was Rick's night off. How could he do this to me? How was I going to react to some new fellow serving as Rick's replacement helping me in the shower. Nope, I will wait for Rick! Well, I wasn't going to have to worry about one of the fellows. In walked one of the best-looking nurses in the hospital to assist me with my shower. Of course, I objected, but there was no way around it. Humility and vanity had been lost the day I broke my back and now I was going to the shower with a woman I didn't even know. Let's call her Penny. She brought with her a metal contraption that looked like a bed frame on wheels. I was stripped of my clothing and rolled onto my left side. "Your incision is healing nicely," she said, cheerfully. I did not respond.

Alongside me she tucked a long sheet which stretched from head to toe. Then I was rolled on the other side and the sheet was pulled underneath me. It was really not a bedsheet, but rather strong nylon mesh net. The bed frame on wheels was rolled up over me and then lowered to bed level. Of course, by now I was covered by a light blanket to protect what remained of my modesty. The outer edges of the mesh net were attached by hook and grommet to the frame and I was hoisted up, just like a fish being lifted from the water.

A lot of work, I thought, *just to get me to the shower only a few feet from my bed. Ohhh, just wait a minute . . . that one is reserved for those who are able to sit while showering.*

So here I was, now being wheeled down the hallway, naked except for the blanket. "Hellooo, Mr. Higginbotham," came a melodic voice from the nurses station as I was ushered by. I didn't respond. *I don't talk to nobody when I'm naked, except for my wife.*

Finally, we were in the shower room, alone. I offered to take my shower with the blanket on, but that didn't work. Darn. Off came the blanket and the shower commenced. Picture a crewman on a ship as he hoses down the deck, and that pretty much describes the scene. My modesty and I recovered fully from that shower, but I did not tell my wife I was in there with a woman I met just minutes before. The shower felt wonderful even if I did not have any sensation from the waist down. The shower was finished and it was time to dry. Just another adventure in rehab land. I asked Penny how I was expected to dry my backside since I could neither sit up, stand up or roll over. "Don't worry," Penny replied. "We will take care of that on the way back." I got covered up, this time with a heavier blanket, and it was back to the room.

"How was your shower, Mr. Higginbotham?"

I thought the greeter would have figured it out from the first time we passed that I don't talk to anyone when I'm naked and especially when I am wet. Penny took me the long way back to the room so the air rushing underneath me could dry my backside. Keep in mind it was February, snowing outside, and the hallways were pretty chilly, but I was completely dry when I reached the room.

The Shrink

I was all cleaned up and ready the next morning to meet the shrink. The meeting went about like I expected it to go—lousy. I didn't want to be there any more than I would have wanted to go to the dentist for a root canal. Furthermore, I was not going to give the shrink any information I thought he might use to analyze me. I don't know what I was thinking or why I had these thoughts. It was some kind of self-defense mechanism, I guess. I told him Devon and I were fine. He needed to talk with my family, but I guess he thought I was trying to blow him off like a nagging fly. I was, but he said he still needed to talk with my family. I did not go into details with the shrink, but the problems I was encountering and observing with some family members were steadily worsening since the accident. I could not understand why they were venting their anger towards me, when I was the one who had been injured. And, although I did not know it at the time, they were making life miserable for Devon as well. I have since learned that this type of situation is not uncommon. However, the stressful exchange is usually between spouses, rather than with other family members.

The shrink asked me all sorts of annoying questions, but one that both puzzled and amused me most was this: He wanted to know what I would do if I was in the Denver airport without any money or credit cards. I asked him if I was supposed to be naked or not. He looked at me funny, but I thought it was a fair question seeing as how over the last two weeks strangers had cut off my favorite hunting pants. Did he know I took a shower with a beautiful nurse I had never seen before? And then she paraded me through the halls wet and naked, covered by only a thin blanket. *Now, Doc, that's something to analyze.*

"Doc, will there be any alien urologists at the airport?" I asked. He did not get my humor, but then he probably has not had my worldly experiences either. I finally answered his question about being stranded in the airport. I said I'd call the office to tell them to wire me some money and that I would be gone for a month.

"Why?" he asked. "Do you have a problem with someone in your office?"

"Nope, I am just going fishing. Hey, Doc, my back is hurting. Can I go now?" I learned early on that I could get out of just about anything with this new excuse. Nobody ever questions a guy with a broken back. The meeting ended up pretty much the same way it began. What ate at me was that he was walking, I was not.

I did get to see the good doctor on a regular basis in group therapy with the rest of the gang each week. During group we were asked to ponder such weighty questions as, "What are you going to do when people stare at you?"

"Heck, people have been staring at me for years. I'm prepared."

After three or four days I was moved to a double room with Chuck because my first room had been too disruptive.

Chuck and I would lie in wait for these special gatherings with the shrink. He and I would find mischief and humor in just about everything during those group sessions. It was our way of coping. All Chuck and I wanted to do was go home and get on with life. We usually brought something bright and funny to our sessions and were always amused at ourselves. Finally, the shrink told us we did not have to attend group therapy meetings anymore. (Now I know where my son gets his sense of humor.)

No Way to Celebrate a Birthday

Soon after their arrival at the spinal center all new patients go through a medical assessment day. The purpose is to outline the therapy routine, to discuss future plans, personal concerns and fears, and to set a goal for a release date (mine was March 10th, and I was actually released a day earlier). My assessment was set for February 9, Devon's birthday. We were both excited and anxious about the meeting. We had the impression it would involve the two of us and the doctor and his staff. Unfortunately, it turned out to be an unexpected family "reunion" and the family was not getting along well as a result of my spinal cord injury.

When I objected to the others attending what was supposed to be a private session with Devon and me, I was treated like I was mentally defective.

Oh well, I thought, *maybe it will help the members of my family to get accustomed to what is going on.* I honestly don't think they realized how important it was for my wife and me to have this meeting alone and in private. It was just another signal that the relationship with my family—some of them my business partners—was worsening and that we were not communicating.

I was annoyed with this unanticipated intrusion, but put on a happy face for the meeting.

Several years later Devon shared with me that no one remembered her birthday. Even me. She even rolled me down to the gift shop in the lobby that day thinking I might be jogged into remembering. As a patient, like I did in business or any other endeavor, I was becoming so focused on myself and my situation that I had overlooked her birthday. I have not forgotten it since then.

Round Wheels in a Square World

My brother and I had been estranged since his high school graduation. He had little contact with most of the family until the declining years of our grandfather's life. However, he did come to the hospital in Dothan right after I was hurt and became a truly wonderful help. Each morning and evening when he and Devon were at Shepherd he would stretch me. (I thought stretching and getting limber was vital to my recovery, and engaged any visitor into helping me with this activity.) It gave us a time to reunite and try out a brotherly routine again. I was very comfortable with the renewal of our relationship and even told him about my conversation with our father and how I forgave him in my heart.

Divorce had seemingly hurt us, the children, more than it had our parents. Now my brother and I were trying to put the pieces back together from our lost childhood.

While I was encouraged about the new relationship with my brother, not long after our conversation things started getting even worse with my mother. The conflict was so bad that with the exception of Devon, the staff restricted the hours my family could observe my therapy. I was relieved by the intervention.

As the family relationships deteriorated, my mother came into my room and told me I could not hold up much longer and that I needed to stop putting on a happy face. She said that I needed to get ahold of myself.

I told her I was really doing fine and I was going to walk one day. What happened next was alarming and shocking. She told me the staff had confided in her and that I would be begging for death before this was over. I know she was under stress, but after she left the room I called my stepfather and told him to come get her. I didn't need to be around anyone or anything negative. He retrieved her and later told me to keep my father away. He said if I planned to bring my father into the picture, or to my home in Plant City, I would regret it.

Knowing there were still bitter feelings over a divorce some three decades earlier, my timing and desire to discuss forgiveness were terrible. All I wanted to do was clear my conscience and make things right. Either way it was a very bad situation for me. So much for a positive and supportive family atmosphere. I would have exchanged 1,000 shower excursions with Penny to have avoided such a confrontation.

Needless to say I did not talk about my father anymore, with anyone. It was bad enough to be in the hospital bed looking up at the fire sprinklers and wondering who would come get me in case of a fire. Now I had to deal with the family dynamics, hatreds and what I perceived as threats. I didn't mention any of this to the shrink. I was afraid he would tell me I had done something wrong by talking with my father.

I know that some of the fears one has after a catastrophic injury are skewed, and that family relationships can change dramatically, but I had a serious problem on my hands. When I mentioned all this to Devon, she began telling me nightmarish stories of her own abusive and demeaning treatment by my family since the accident. How could this be? My family was coming apart at the seams. I was not at the end of my rope—it had already slipped from my hands. I copped out. I dumped on my wife, and told her to handle her problems herself because my system was overloaded. It was. I urinated through a tube, my bowel movement was extracted in an unspeakable manner, I had been told my sex life was on permanent hold and, by the way, "You won't walk again." I didn't need any of this. I was wrong telling Devon that she would have to deal with her problems herself, but there was no way out. We did not speak of the family problems again until I returned home.

Another Subtle Reminder

That evening after my medical review, Devon and I went down to the chapel located on the main floor at Shepherd. It was a small and beautiful setting where I often sought privacy and found refuge. Just like the night before the hunting trip, I found a Bible provided by the Gideons. It brought me relief as I sought passages for comfort. When I traveled, I had always left my own Bible at home in a safe place. It was kept on the coffee table for easy access and within view, just in case my pastor stopped by for a visit. This was the last trip I made without it.

Despite the overwhelming problems with my family, Devon and I were determined to stay close during my rehab. She set up house in Atlanta while waiting for an opening in one of the town houses within walking distance of Shepherd. The town houses had been donated for the use of families of patients on a first-come basis. Meanwhile Devon's sister, Candi, who lived in Plantation, Florida, moved into our home in Plant City to care for our children. She returned to her own home only once, the weekend the children came to visit me.

While the pressure and uncertainty must have been tremendous for her, Devon never missed a step as she lived the "for better or worse" part of our wedding vows. Soon after her move she was at the rehab center every day. She looked great and was always in excellent spirits. That night when we went to the chapel to talk, we began recapping the weeks since my accident. She told me of her proclamation: "Al will walk again." I was dumbfounded. I had never told her about my prayer to God while I was still pinned under the tree. We were both excited and knew this was yet another reminder from God about what really happened that day.

Both of us knew I wasn't going to leave Shepherd walking, but we set goals for my progress, which included going back to Glacier National Park in Montana, and hiking to Grinnell Glacier. This was a hike we had made on several occasions and we both knew it would be something we could do again. I could visualize the spectacular landscape and the trails.

I was so excited by our mutual revelation—our belief that I would walk—that upon returning to my room I shared it with some of the staff. They did not receive my revelation in quite the same manner and talked to me again about "denial." From then on I kept my goals to myself.

My roommate, Charlie, also offered support. He was just what I needed for strength and inspiration. In fact, Charlie will be my hero forever. I think we fed off one another. Charlie had been on a hunting trip and while returning home had a car accident and broke his neck. If he could make it, I knew I could. He was getting dressed, shaving, bathing without assistance and was one of the first patients to arrive in the dining room at meal time. Through his help, I figured out how to get my britches on without an audience—mainly my occupational therapist—and life started to go on.

C HAPTER

Life at a Spinal Center

The way I see it, if you want the rainbow,
you gotta put up with the rain.—Dolly Parton

The newspaper and television news carried many examples of personal tragedies, which I always followed to some extent with morbid curiosity. Now, here I sat in the center of heartbreak. Could I possibly be one of them now? As I met other patients, I was able to put names, faces, voices, tears and laughter with many of the stories I had so often read.

The Shepherd Spinal Center was a truly wonderful facility, despite my occasional comments to the contrary. The staff worked under tremendous pressure, taking in the worst kind of injuries a person could ever suffer—spinal cord and closed head injuries. They save lives but more important they help the injured and family members put the pieces back together. I am eternally grateful for everything they did for me—especially putting up with this smart-mouth country boy from Plant City. I have in the past and will continue to refer patients and families to Shepherd. Recently, I was asked to sit on its National Advisory Board.

Blessing in Disguise

While there, I realized I did not have to look very far to find someone who was in a lot worse shape than I was. This was not a place to feel sorry for yourself, but too often others do so for you. What left a distinct impression on my mind were the faces of my visitors. My room was at the end of the hall and my visitors would have to pass by many rooms that were so full of tragedy. One of my guests became ill and had to leave. After their long walk to my room I greeted them, usually from my bed, and fifty pounds lighter than I had been before the accident, with a big smile. I tried to reassure them that everything was okay. I had become accustomed to my surroundings, but to a first-time visitor the center was a real eye-opener.

Slowly I was becoming institutionalized. One clear sign that I was in an institution was the day the housekeeping staff came to do my laundry. I wanted to know how they were going to keep my underwear separate from the others. "Oh, Mr. Higginbotham, don't worry. We wrote your name in all your clothing."

Oh no! I thought, and immediately called Devon who was taking a break at home with the children. "Honey, they have put my name in all my undershorts. Send me my good ones and quick. You know— my Jockey shorts without the holes in them—and run them through a bleach cycle as well."

I wasn't into making a fashion statement in my underwear, especially in my condition, but I didn't want anybody knowing that I wore underwear with holes. I got new underwear and threw away my comfy old familiars. Case closed.

During my junior and senior years in high school I was active in a service organization called Key Club. Our international theme was "Influence Through Example." There were some patients who had a profound influence on me at Shepherd. Brave faces stood tall at Shepherd. There were many shining examples of humanity mixed in with cases of inhumanity. There was young Sally, a high school student. During the Christmas vacation, her boyfriend, who was despondent over their breakup, took a high-powered hunting rifle to the Christmas parade, aimed at her head and shot her, before turning the gun on himself and committing suicide. He missed Sally's head, but the bullet ripped through her neck, leaving her paralyzed from the neck down. In the beginning she was unable to talk, or even breathe on her own.

I was there when she learned to talk again, and witnessed the frightening task of learning to breathe without the assistance of a ventilator. As we passed one another in the halls, her beautiful eyes happy, she gave me reassurance I needed. I hoped my smile was a gesture-in-kind as well.

Dwayne was paralyzed from the waist down. He had fallen out of the bucket of a front-end loader while trimming trees in his yard. His eyes were sad and he longed for the day he would return home to his sons. He found such great happiness in sharing success stories of his sons.

And then there was another young man, Chester, who broke his neck while diving off a bridge. He would sit in his room with his headset on as he listened to gospel music and sang aloud with the tune.

As I would roll down the hall I would peer into the room of a priest who was on what I figured to be life-support. I was told a drunk driver put him there.

There were too many young people who had been shot accidentally in there . The last time I saw Tuyen he was so despondent he was trying to figure a way to take his life. He asked me for help. We had all survived some life-shattering and changing events, but nothing could ever be bad enough to take your life. Although I sparred and exchanged jabs with the shrink, I contacted him right away and expressed my concerns for my friend.

The most memorable comment made was that of an African-American man, Abraham, who had been hit by a car. He was paralyzed from the shoulders down and had lost an eye as a result of the accident. His parting statement to me the day he was released to go home was, "The lights are out at the disco, but I ain't leaving." My heart was moved and forever strengthened by having the privilege of living with these Trojans of tragedy.

I was getting better and started to think about going home.

Homesick

Go up to your fears and speak to them, and they will generally fade away. — A. MacLaren, D.D.

Five weeks had passed since the accident. I hadn't seen my children since Dothan, and Devon was planning a big weekend visit with them at Shepherd. We felt it was important for the kids to see me before I returned home. Their father would be coming home in a wheelchair and we wanted to get all their questions and fears behind us—as best we could. They needed to see where dad had spent his time since leaving the hospital in Dothan. My immediate concern was that I would become overwhelmed with emotion when I saw them, but I didn't. I fought back the tears of joy when Allen and Kaylon walked into my room. I could not get over how much they had changed. They were very excited to see me.

The time away from them had been a blur. I had not only missed Allen's first basketball game, I missed the entire season. Kaylon's first riding lesson—well, I missed that as well. It still would be six months before I would see her ride a horse. Never again, I promised myself, never again would I put my personal or business needs before my wife and children. The weekend visit passed too quickly.

Astonishingly, while they were very excited and all eyes, they did not seem to be unduly distressed by my condition or the surroundings. Kaylon wanted to ride in my wheelchair and Allen brought me a sack full of get-well cards made by his schoolmates. Their attitude, and that of their friends, was marvelous and their humor a delight.

The children and their friends continued to be a source of joy, and their observations, stories, and comments made me smile in the hospital and much later when I was back home.

I had not been home from Shepherd very long and was cooking on the grill for some of Kaylon's friends. I overheard one of them commenting about the small size of the hamburgers. Another child piped up in my defense and said, "Kaylon's dad can't help it, he's handicapped."

When I came home I was unable to go upstairs to our bedrooms, so we were revising our family fire drill. The kids have an escape ladder in each of their rooms and I asked them what they would do

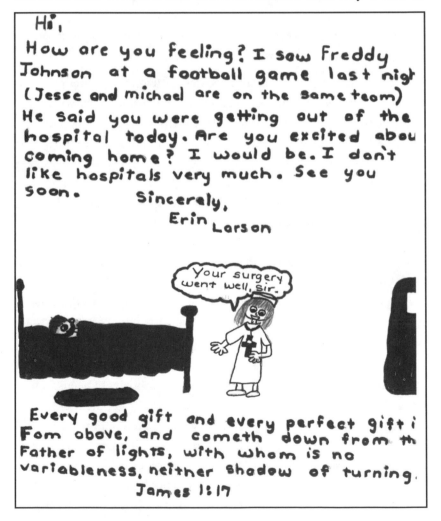

and say in the event they smelled smoke. Kaylon wryly replied, "Good-bye, Dad."

* * *

On the facing page is one of the many letters I cherish from my children's friends. Above, Kaylon used her artistic talents to create a very special get-well card, with a colorful front and back.

That first weekend visit with my kids was over all too soon. I became homesick and was ready to leave, so I refocused my attention to my therapy.

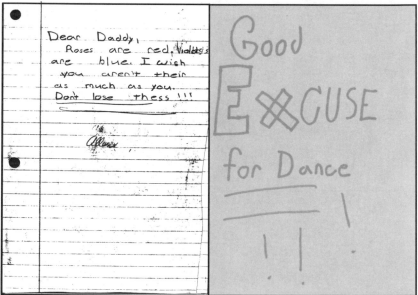

Allen also had some very touching messages for me. And he has a great sense of humor! He knew I was looking for an excuse to stop taking ballroom dancing lessons with Devon.

I began counting the days and crossing them off on my calendar as March 9th, my new projected release date, approached. I started getting a burning electrical shocking sensation in my left leg. The pain was similar to what I had experienced in the woods the day the tree fell on me, but not as severe. I thought maybe my legs were trying to wake up, but I wasn't sure. The quadriceps in my right leg started to flicker. I could pull my left leg up by sliding my foot on the bed pointing my knee skyward. It was an exhausting effort as I broke into a sweat. But I didn't have the muscle control to balance so it just flopped over. The doctor showed little interest and discounted this progress, telling me I would need my hips and knees working if I ever hoped to walk. He said he was not real encouraged by the return of sensation. It did not matter. I was pleased and that was all that counted.

Joys of an Insurance Adjuster

Sometimes dealing with an adjuster is like being asked over to a dinner at someone's home only to learn they are on a fat-free diet and think you should be, too! I was tiring of the staff and Shepherd as my attention now was focused on going home. Our house needed to be modified, doctors lined up, and a physical therapist had to be located. I learned through the staff at Shepherd that my insurance adjuster would be assigning a case manager to assist me with all the big decisions regarding my future and health care. This was a standard procedure in catastrophic injuries like mine, but I did not like the thought of people poking their noses in my private business.

When Devon and I built our house in 1991, we made most of it wheelchair accessible, thinking one day, when we were old, one of us might need one. Now, when we began planning house modifications we learned the family had already made the changes they felt were necessary. We were told by those involved with the modifications that we were too caught up in our problems, that we didn't know what we were doing, and that the work was complete. I am usually grateful for help, but when it is not done correctly and to proper wheelchair specifications, it can spell disaster and did. Later when I tried to have the problems corrected, I was told by the adjuster all necessary modifications had been completed. I was very frustrated.

The problems with the insurance company did not end there. I explained to my insurance adjuster and new case manager that I wanted a male therapist and doctor. I knew there were capable females in the profession, but with the complex and personal nature of my injury, I knew I would relate better to a guy.

I had already stripped for Penny in the shower and had been examined by the alien urologists. I wanted to make some of my own decisions now. It was several weeks after I returned home that I met my new doctor. To my dismay, my request for a male doctor was ignored and I found myself on the examination table with yet another stranger. The female doctor and I never developed a relationship.

The doctor practiced medicine in constant fear of the insurance company. It is a sad commentary, but too often the case in today's modern medical management. I would learn even more about the role the insurance company would play in my life and health care.

Another Prayer Answered

While still at Shepherd, I began praying for a therapist who would take me on as a special project when I was discharged from the facility. I wanted someone whose eyes would not glaze over when I told him I planned to walk again. The prayer was answered. A deacon in my church by the name of Keith Kolakowski was to be my new therapist. When first approached, Keith declined. He confided in my friend, Freddy, that there were too many problems with cases like mine and he did not want to get involved. Fred told him, "You don't know Al. He is different," and talked Keith into taking me on as one of his patients. Thanks, Fred.

CHAPTER 11

Going Home

The best and most beautiful things in the world cannot be seen or even heard. They must be felt with the heart.—Helen Keller

Jenny Craig, you can throw away the control-top pantyhose and your weight-loss diet because I have found a new way to lose weight. My last full day at Shepherd followed a typical check-out routine including a stop at the scales. I hadn't noticed it, but I was pretty bony. The scales showed that I had lost forty-seven pounds since breaking my back—weighing in now at 148 pounds. You can do the math because I'm not admitting to anyone just exactly how much I weighed back in January when I had gone on that hunting trip and had the accident. It occurred to me that we should rename this place the Shepherd Spinal Center and Weight-Loss Clinic.

My last night at the spinal center, my nurse, Bob, stopped by to wish me well. He told me I was going home with something many, others were not going home to: hope. He was impressed with Devon and our positive attitude. Another staffer came in and asked me if I was scared. "No, I am just excited and eager." I was beginning to feel and think institutionalized and was ready to make a break for it. People were talking to me as if I were sick and feeble. I had no privacy and what I wanted and missed most was some of that. As I was checking my bags, I wondered if I had all my underwear. It doesn't matter now, I thought, if someone sees a pair of Jockeys with my name in them. They'll think that Higginbotham guy is all right. Just look at the good undershorts he wears!

By now I was bathing myself and was taking a shower when the door opened slowly. "Mr. Higginbotham are you in there?"

Who would it be? Some doctor, or maybe a homeless guy is stealing an opportunity to take a bath in my bathroom?

"Come in."

It was my occupational therapist; I recognized her voice. She was checking to make sure I was doing okay in the shower by myself. I had gotten used to the intrusions and it did not matter who came in. I was bathing with my shorts on. One naked shower early on at the center was enough for this old country boy from Plant City. I knew my next shower would be a real one with my clothes off and hot water. For safety reasons the temperature has to be turned down at the center to avoid having a patient burn him or herself.

After my shower I turned in, knowing that the next night I wouldn't have a hospital intercom at the head of my bed. There would be no alarms signaling a ventilator needed checking, no muffled tears of some family member, no early morning aliens. I was so wound up I asked for a sleeping pill to get me through the night.

Wheels up for Home

Friday morning, March 9, after checking out of Shepherd, Devon and I were in a taxi headed for the Atlanta airport. In the cab I read a message, marked urgent, which was delivered to me earlier in the morning. It was from my case manager at the insurance company. I was supposed to call before I left the hospital. Maybe she was calling to wish me well. That would be nice since she had not been very friendly. Maybe I won a door prize. Maybe they were going to send me flowers. I waited until I was at the airport before returning her call. I identified myself and this creep, otherwise known as my case manager, tore into me, telling me I had no authorization to leave the hospital and if I didn't return immediately I would forfeit my benefits. I tried to reason with her and finally, without saying good-bye, I hung up on her. Until that call I had never hung up on anyone during a phone conversation. I never heard from her again and the insurance company *did pay* the bill.

Even though Devon was with me, making my way through the Atlanta airport was an unsettling experience. I was very apprehensive about boarding an airplane as a paraplegic. I was already on edge after leaving the security of the "institution," and now I was boarding an aircraft full of people. It was more than I wanted to deal with my first hours away from the center. The call was made for those needing assistance to board now. The gate attendant assured me that I would be boarded first using an aisle chair, and then the airline personnel would lift me into my seat. The gate attendant told me to wait, and then she forgot about me. I asked, "Shouldn't I board first?"

"Just wait," the woman at the counter said to me. The last thing I wanted to do was appear helpless on a plane full of people. I was to be boarded last. I didn't want to get on the plane. Devon said, "Come on, the kids are waiting to see you."

I had no choice. With a lump in my throat I thought, This is my first real venture "outside." I dug deep, mustering the dignity I needed to get on the plane with assistance. As they were placing me in my seat, the attendant asked me if I wanted him to put my wheelchair cushion on the seat, saying that I would be more comfortable.

I said, "No, I don't need my wheelchair cushion underneath me. Don't put it there."

"Oh, sir," he insisted, "you will be more comfortable with your own cushion."

The cushion ended up on my seat anyway, and I sat a head above everyone else. I felt as though I looked like a basketball player—with no place to hide.

Devon told me that many of our friends had wanted to come to the Tampa airport to greet us when we arrived. I, however, wanted my return to be a private family affair. No, I wasn't bothered by anyone seeing me in a wheelchair. I just wanted to be alone with Devon and the children. I did not want any distractions my first evening home. So only my children and their grandparents were there to pick us up.

Something wonderful happened as I was getting off the plane. Looking back, I am glad I didn't have a larger welcoming committee. I experienced a sensation—it's one we all have several times a day— an urge to go to the bathroom and it was a call of immediacy. Maybe it was a nervous response, but all I know was that my bladder had been in the "off" position since my accident and this was a welcome sign of relief. Right there at Tampa International Airport I peed in my pants. I went into the rest room and found I could not get my chair into the stall to finish off the experience by catheterization. Devon found a security guard, who in turn summoned a custodian. The custodian cleared out the men's rest room and secured the door so I could make sure the mission was complete by using the catheter. Hey, I had wet my pants, but something below my waist was starting to work again! It was necessary to wear extra padding for quite some time while I relearned some of life's basics.

There Is No Place Like Home

When I arrived home, I rolled from room to room downstairs, just looking around.

"Open the windows," I said. "The orange blossoms are beginning to bloom and I want to smell them. I want to hear the trains as they pass by tonight."

Then I realized that bedtime was nearing. Who was going to turn me over tonight? Would I need any of those other nighttime intrusions and checks that I had grown accustomed to while in the hospital? For the last couple of months the hospital staff would come in and turn me over as needed to prevent pressure sores. Tonight, for the first time since my accident, I was on my own. I would use the guest room downstairs until I was strong enough to bump myself up each step to the second floor. (Bumping is a type of transfer in which you get out of your wheelchair and sit on the steps, pulling up with your arms until reaching the top of the stairs.)

Devon and I had already agreed she would continue to sleep upstairs to keep continuity with the children. We knew it could be months before I was strong enough to bump myself up the steps at night. In fact, it was five months before I was strong enough to make it to the second floor. Meanwhile, I had a cowbell to ring if I needed help. Oddly enough, I didn't feel vulnerable, but I worried that I could not respond to my family if they needed help. We bought a secondhand wheelchair for me to use upstairs. What a joy it was to finally make it upstairs to my bed for a night's sleep.

The last thing we did that first night before going to bed was to cut off my blue hospital wristband. At my request, according to a plan

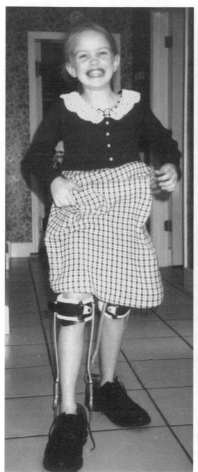 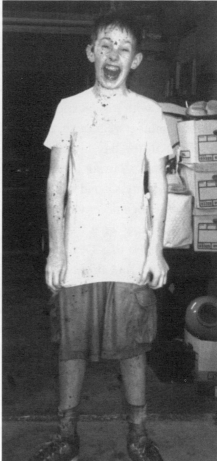

The kids adjusted just fine to their dad's disability and recovery. (Left) Kaylon tried wearing my new braces. And, Allen, wet and covered with mud, soon got back to his routine.

I made at Shepherd, I asked Devon to thumbtack my hospital wristband high on the inside of the door trim in the guest room. It could only be reached by standing. One day, yes, one day I would stand up and remove the wristband myself.

It was nearly midnight when we all got settled. Devon went upstairs to bed with the kids and I rolled into the guest bathroom. I had to see if my plumbing was working so I transferred to the toilet to take a try. Rats! No luck! So back to the catheter.

On my first morning home I slept until 7:45 A.M. I spent time riding around the farm on the golf cart. Everything looked good. I did not realize how much I missed home. Freddy and Tammy Johnson were my first visitors that morning. I told him about my visit in the woods from God and how He had answered my prayer that day. I told Fred I was going to return to Glacier National Park and hike up to Grinnell Glacier again. It was important for me to set goals and to share them with trusted friends, even though we didn't talk about the hike for another year or so. Fred said, "Count me in."

Later in the day my pastor came by and he was followed by a string of guests lasting late into the night.

Sunday, my second full day home, Allen seemed to be adjusting just fine. He came downstairs, turned the television on loudly and wanted to know what I was making him for breakfast. This was terrific. I insisted that Devon and the kids go to church, telling her I would be just fine alone.

Solitude and quiet were something I had not experienced since my injury. I could not wait to be alone, but when they left, it hit me like a brick wall. I was overwhelmed as I rolled through the house and into my office. I stared at my desk. What was I going to do? There was tension with my stepfather and mother and we were in business together. The kids needed braces. One day they would need money to go to college. I knew I would be okay, but I had been away for almost two months and the world did not stop while I was in the hospital. Where and how would I restart?

By the time Devon came home she found me in a sorry state.

"Not on my watch," she said, as she rolled me outside into the sunlight and fresh air. It was amazing how simple things in life can make a difference. It had been years since I simply sat outside for no particular purpose other than to enjoy Mother Nature. Even when I hunted I was on a mission. I could not remember what it was like just to sit and enjoy the moment.

Keith's First Visit

It's not whether you get knocked down; it's whether you get up again.
—Vince Lombardi

It was March 16th. I had been home one week now and I was enjoying my newfound freedom. Devon and Kaylon had gone into town to run some errands so it was just Allen and me at home waiting for the physical therapist to arrive for my first session.

Getting dressed on my own was still a difficult task so I paced myself when getting ready every morning. I usually did not sit around in my undershorts, but this morning Mr. Modesty was doing just that. (I knew they are my undershorts because my name had been inked into the waistband at the hospital.) The therapist showed up thirty minutes early and Allen, not thinking anything about dad sitting in the living room in his Jockeys, let him in without even telling me that we had a visitor. In a less-than-friendly manner, I kicked Keith out of my house until the scheduled time. Unknown to me, he sat in his car in the driveway until I was ready. What a jerk he must have thought I was! Anybody else would have left, wished me good luck and never come back. When I let him back in, he apologized and told me when this was over we would end up being close friends. He was right.

He passed my first test when I told him about my prayer and the visit from God while I was pinned under the tree. He did not look at me in disbelief nor did he refer me to a shrink. I was relieved and figured we were going to get along just fine.

"Okay," he said. "Let's get to work and see what you can do."

Close Your Eyes and Imagine

Initially he came to my house to work with me six days a week. From the eyes of the professional, I'm sure it didn't appear that I had much to work with, except hope and profound faith. I remember him telling me, "As I move your legs for you, imagine your nerves are reconnecting and commanding your muscle to work." That was how my home therapy began, with imagination. This would continue for the next three years, although in time I had only three sessions a week.

Learning to walk is no different for an adult than it is for a baby. The first order of business was be limber. Babies come limber; adults don't. Keith made sure I was limber by giving me stretching exercises to do between sessions. I rose early each morning and treated my therapy as if it were my job, which it was. I dedicated myself totally to the therapy program. As I grew stronger, I was able to go to his office and he worked with me during his lunch hour. I don't think I comprehended his sacrifice at the time, but he selflessly helped me both at my home and at his office. Oh how God had answered my prayer for a therapist!

Something's Wrong

As the weeks passed I noticed something was happening with my legs. Painful electrical shocks, similar to what I experienced the day I was injured, were circulating throughout my lower body, and my skin was increasingly painful to the touch. Could it be that I was not used to sleeping on anything but hospital sheets? One of the cruel tricks and misconceptions of paralysis is that even if you are void of any sensation you still experience pain. I was no exception. The pain intensified with time, often reducing me to tears.

I had been home three months when I knew that something was terribly wrong with my back. I felt like I had a swarm of angry hornets under my skin, stinging me over and over. As I moved I could feel and hear bones crunching and grinding in my back. I made an unscheduled visit to the doctor's office. I insisted something was wrong, and although I was not due for X rays until the following month, I wanted them now. I told her that I wanted to know what was wrong, even if I had to pay for the X rays myself. My hunch was right. The films revealed a serious problem and she referred me to a neurosurgeon.

Take Control

An appointment was set and a week later I waited for the neurosurgeon to come into the examination room. He entered and with an arrogant and rude manner, acted as if I were imposing on his valuable time. I thought he was getting paid to do this and that he would be happy to see another customer. He told me, "Congratulations, your fusion has failed and surgery is necessary." The surgeon said he would enter my spine, making a point to tell me, single-handedly with an anterior (from the front) incision, setting aside my internal organs to get to the job site and he then would repair the damage.

Here was this jerk, treating me as if I were less than intelligent as he told me how he was going to conduct the operation. I had already made up my mind that this guy was never going to touch me with a knife. He was offended when I told him I wanted a second opinion. "Suit yourself," he said. "You will be back!"

He had discovered the failed fusion and seemed to think that it was his right to operate on me. But, no doctor was operating on my back by going through my belly, especially if I didn't like him. I left his office knowing I would never return as his patient.

Summer Plans and Goals are Interrupted

The kids were out of school for the summer and this is not what I had in mind—terrible pain and physical degeneration. What of the goals I was setting? Could I ever function again? The insurance adjuster was dragging her feet, so I set an appointment myself for another evaluation, knowing that insurance would not pay for the visit. The next neurosurgeon I saw agreed with the urgency of surgery, but said it was too complex and risky a surgery for him to undertake. He referred me to another neurologist at Shands Hospital at the University of Florida in Gainesville. An appointment was set, but the next opening was six months away. The receptionist told me to feel free to call back every day to see if there was a cancellation and then maybe she could work me into the schedule. I called every day as my condition worsened. The pain was intensifying and the pain medication did not help.

Meanwhile, Jamie Paternally, my college classmate and Sigma Chi fraternity brother, learned of my plight. Jamie, a surgeon in Houston, Texas, routinely operates on catastrophic injury patients with a couple of neurosurgeons and orthopedic surgeons. He discussed my case with them and they fortunately found it interesting. These surgeons had an idea for relieving my pain and for providing my spine with necessary room to heal. And maybe, this would help me be able to "ambulate." (We don't say "walk," because, remember I am a paraplegic.)

Fast Action

Jamie called me on a Wednesday to say he wanted my films and any records as soon as possible. That meant I would have to get my records from the jerk of a doctor in Tampa. Unbelievably, I succeeded that very same day and sent them by overnight mail to Houston. On Friday I received a call from the offices of Dr. David Baskin, the neurosurgeon, and Dr. Jeff Kozak, an orthopedic surgeon, asking if I could be in their Houston office first thing on Monday. Here I was on a six-month waiting list at Shands, but my connections in Houston had worked. Monday morning? I wasn't sure how I was going to make the trip. I wanted Devon there for the evaluation, but there was no one to watch the kids. The decision, however, was easy and immediate. I told the receptionist I would be there.

We could not afford to fly all of us, but quickly determined it was a seventeen-hour drive. So, on Saturday morning, August 19, we loaded up the van and headed to Houston. The first stop would be New Orleans and then it would be an easy five-hour drive on Sunday. Although this trip was a very serious mission we treated it like a mini-vacation. The last several months had been tough on everyone and a break in New Orleans was just the answer. Devon and the children enjoyed the sights while I found myself an unintentional panhandler on street corners or outside shops that were not wheelchair accessible. You think I am kidding? Put me on any street corner in the country in a wheelchair and people offer me money. One of the benefits of being in a wheelchair is that the real panhandlers leave you alone—professional courtesy I guess.

On Sunday evening we arrived at the Hilton located at the medical center and checked into our room. I was doing all this without the prior approval of my insurance adjuster, knowing that I was responsible for all expenses. I called Jamie at home on Sunday night to let him know we had arrived. We planned dinner the next evening at his house. I had not seen him for nearly twenty years and was most grateful for his unsolicited help and hospitality.

The next morning I saw Dr. Jeff Kozak, the orthopedic surgeon, and then later I met with the neurosurgeon, Dr. David Baskin. They had a plan that involved a team of four surgeons and about eight hours of their handiwork in the operating room. It would require removing my damaged vertebrae and, in their place, using a femur to span the distance. A femur, where do you plan to get the femur? I wanted to know. They said it would come from an organ donor and was referred to as allograft. The operation was considered high-tech and risky, but I was in pain and, more importantly, I wanted to walk again. I had some misgivings about the transplant side of the operation until I later researched the process and was satisfied that this was the right choice.

Jumping the Span

The next stop was to go back home and call the insurance adjuster. Our last conversation had been when I hung up on her while I was at the airport in Atlanta. I figured, well, if you are going to burn your bridges be prepared to jump the span. And that's exactly what I had to do. I ran various possible conversations through my mind, and then called her, trying to smooth things out and get the approvals that I needed.

I can't remember where we left off when we were last talking . . . . How's the family? . . . Oh, me, I'm fine . . . just got back from Houston to see some doctors. Yes, Houston. . . No, the one in Texas. I paid for the trip and the visits with the doctors. . . . No, I did not get authorization. . . . Yes, I understand you will not reimburse me for these reckless and irresponsible actions I have taken.

She didn't have to scold me. I knew what I was doing—trying to walk again. All I wanted her to do was approve the surgery, which was already set for November 1.

Well you see this fraternity brother knows these guys who are surgeons and they have an idea about a surgical procedure. I'm sure they have tried it before, I continued.

"Ooohh, a Sigma Chi fraternity brother? That's different," said the adjuster.

I think you get the idea of how my conversation was going—downhill. She said she would get back to me and reminded me that I would not be reimbursed for the doctors' evaluations in Houston.

A few days passed and I called her again. I faxed and wrote the adjuster only to find out that she had been replaced. Great! I guessed they were bringing out the big guns. You know the feeling you get when you know you are being ignored? I had that feeling. Finally, I heard from my new adjuster. I had to start the story all over again. This new adjuster responded no differently. "I will get back with you," she said. She didn't, but, instead, had my caseworker call me. "When do you want to schedule the surgery and, by the way, did you keep your receipts? We have agreed to pay your travel expenses as well as the medical visits. We will even pay for your wife to travel with you. By the way, if your wife will help you after surgery while you are recovering at the hotel we will pay her instead of a home health nurse," the caseworker told me. I was astonished. God works in amazing ways.

Everything was set and I was Houston-bound for surgery on November 1, 1995. Between now and then I had to prepare myself mentally and physically for the operation. (This included several visits to the blood banks to store up my own blood as the team anticipated quite a bit of blood loss during the operation.) The Houston doctors were going to go through my belly, just like the first surgeon had recommended, but because of their attitude and plans, I did not mind these guys doing it.

Crisis within a Crisis—I Really Needed This
When I first entered Shepherd Spinal Center, I learned the divorce rate was extremely high for people with spinal cord injuries. It was considered just another problem to deal with after suffering such a debilitating injury. Keep in mind every ounce of self-confidence and grit is exposed and tested, every emotion is stretched, ripped and torn from the inside. The trauma caused by a catastrophic injury affects every family member, causing the best and worst to surface in everyone involved. My family was no exception.

Devon and I had a good marriage before I was injured. In our case, the spinal cord injury served as an instrument to strengthen our relationship, bringing the best to the top. It gave us a wonderful opportunity under the worst of circumstances to spend more time together. The same went for our children. I looked at the post-hospital period as an opportunity to remake myself both physically and personally. For me it was a time to get closer to God and reestablish lost relationships with those that had fallen by the wayside. It didn't always work that way. Devon and I were becoming increasingly aware that some people were not handling my spinal cord injury and disability very well. While it was often the spouse who backed out of the marriage, in my case the "divorce" was with certain family members— those with whom I had been in business. The timing of the unexpected "divorce" and the way it was handled, for whatever reasons, was very stressful.

Although there were many warning signals before I left Shepherd, I had been home less than two weeks in March when the fireworks began. One of my partners came to my home and told me that he did not want to be in business with me any more, saying I was different now. I was half a man. Looking around the room, I saw there were only the two of us and I was the only one sitting in a wheelchair, so I figured he was talking about me. After months of discussion, mostly heated and mean-spirited, I knew there was little hope that I, as a disabled person, would be accepted back into my family business. This would prove to be a test even more difficult to handle than suffering a spinal cord injury.

The emerging business/family environment was heartbreaking, unnecessary and it diverted much of my attention away from the most important task I had ever faced—overcoming paralysis and learning to walk again. Later, when events became clear, we had another meeting at my home. I pleaded for time—just a little more time . . . just a few moments over the span of a lifetime to be able to focus on my recovery. This was viewed as selfish and self-centered by my business partner.

At this point I had been home less than three weeks and had been reading a copy of Dennis Byrd's book *Rise and Walk* in which he wrote about the importance of totally focusing your mission on recovery. But my plea for more time was met with profanity as my partners stormed out of my house. I yelled, "Don't leave, come back." I could not follow them. My wheelchair had been taken to another room and I was left sitting, helpless, in an easy chair in the living room.

As I dragged myself into the dining room to retrieve my wheelchair my mind swirled with confusion. My tears were of frustration, anger, embarrassment, fear and uncertainty. How was I ever going to get through this? Would I ever be able to provide for my family again?

I had the bright idea of getting everybody together for personal counseling. That's the code word for going to the shrink, even though I had avoided such help while I was at Shepherd. I wondered if my partner was correct and that the accident had not only left me physically handicapped, but also mentally incapable of handling anything for myself again. With my confidence shaken, I was convinced I was the problem and so I faithfully went to the psychologist for nearly a year. At first I asked my business partners/family to attend these therapy sessions with me, but they refused, telling me I was the one with the mental shortcomings. Finally, I wrote a letter asking them to attend counseling. The letter was returned to me. I was brokenhearted. I wrote two more letters and they were returned unopened. I wasn't catching on yet but kept on trying. This was worse than the evening the doctor told me I would never walk again. I knew one day I would prevail over this terrible paralysis and I wanted so much for my family to be a part of my victory. But, under the circumstances, I knew this would never happen.

A Christian psychologist in Lakeland was a tremendous help during the time I was in therapy with him. I learned from him that I was not the problem. In fact, I was handling the psychological problems related to the paralysis pretty well. To this day I can honestly say that I was never depressed as a result of the injury—aggravated and frustrated, yes, but not depressed. On the other hand, I had a lot of difficulty understanding the family fallout as a result of my spinal cord injury.

Eventually the family business would be sold. After a year of negations and pleading, I was left with no alternative but to seek legal counsel to collect my portion of the proceeds. Meanwhile, Devon and I had gone from a three-car family to a no-car family. Keeping a roof over our heads had become a serious concern. Our funds and finances

I missed Kaylon's first horseback riding lesson, but I was there for her first show. Showing off her blue and yellow ribbons, we were making up for time lost.

After basketball season, Allen ran the mile race on Spring Olympics Day. He wore my old track shirt from high school in Plant City.

were intermingled in the family business and I had a wife and children to provide for and a paralysis to beat. I was determined to do both. It was only after careful thought and prayer that I made the toughest decision of my life. I filed suit. I did not pick this fight, but took the first swing. My eyes had fallen upon a passage in the Bible and I acted accordingly.

Proverbs 17:1: *Better a dry crust with peace and quiet than a house full of feasting with strife* (NIV).

I could write an entire book about this tragic twist within a tragic time of my life, but this book is about victory and happiness. We often say there are two sides to a story, but I think it is more accurate to say there are many sides to any story and our tragic fallout is no exception.

Looking back at the sad period I have no doubt these events severely affected my ability to focus completely on my recovery, and wonder where I would be if I did not have this terrible distraction.

Keeping Promises

There is no self-made man. You reach your goals only with the help of others. — George Shinn

Setting Goals

During the remainder of the summer of 1995 my physical and emotional hands were full. I had challenges and was often sent a subtle reminder that God had paid me a visit while I lay critically injured under that tree in the woods. I knew I had to uphold my end of the bargain through hard work, perseverance, but most importantly, by setting goals. Early on, Devon and I made plans to go back to Glacier National Park and again hike to Grinnell Glacier, and it was time to set both short- and long-range goals as well. Besides, our personal plans would help divert my attention from the family/business problems.

I began setting goals early on during my stay at Shepherd. I had met my first, which was to be released from the spinal center one day sooner than expected. Others weren't as easy at the time. I am an avid NASCAR fan and always held a "500" party if we were not at the race itself. That February was different. I watched the Daytona 500 by myself at Shepherd, but I vowed that I would be in Daytona for the Pepsi 400 race during the summer.

I was active in the Hillsborough County Republican Party, and secretly wanted to get home in time to attend the annual fund-raiser on March 31. I promised myself that I would take Devon and my children camping at Indian Creek in the Smoky Mountain National Park during the summer of 1995. I told myself daily that I would one day walk again. I promised myself I would go hunting again during the upcoming deer season. I promised myself I would live up to all the expectations of my wife and children. Recalling Psalm 76:28, *But as for me it is good to be near God. I have made the sovereign Lord my refuge; I will tell of all your deeds. (NIV)* I made a personal vow to tell all of God's deeds in delivering me from paralysis.

Hillsborough County Lincoln Day dinner, March 31, 1995. Just ten weeks after the accident, and almost fifty pounds lighter, I was there, displaying the award that had been presented to me by the Republican Party and candidate Jeb Bush.

Goals are very important. They give definition and reason to all the hard work and sometimes meaningless detail that are necessary for success. I never could have endured those countless hours of therapy if I had not focused on Grinnell Glacier.

I made it out of Shepherd early and attended the Lincoln Day Dinner just two weeks after coming home. However, I had not planned for the evening to turn out as it did. I was the honoree and the Man of the Year. (I would have broken my back sooner if I had known I would get this kind of recognition.) The following year, 1996, I walked to the podium of the Lincoln Day fund-raiser dinner, not only to say thanks, but because I was the chairman of the event.

Daytona's Pepsi 400

I had not missed Daytona's 400-mile race since 1979, and was not sure I would be able to make the race in July 1995. Here I was in the middle of a terrible family/business dispute, broke and full of self-

Among those
joining me at the
Daytona 400 were
my physical
therapist Keith
Kolakowski and his
daughter, Lauren.

I did not waste
any time becoming
active once again.
Devon and I
attended the
Rainbow Ball in
April 1995.

doubt. I did not bother to buy tickets for the race. At the last minute, however, my therapist and friend, Fred, talked me into going. On race day I was flanked by Keith, Fred, and our children at the newly constructed backstretch grandstand as we purchased tickets. I wheeled around to the ramp and proceeded to our assigned seats. There was an area at track level reserved for wheelchair users, but I passed it by, instead heading for our seats in the grandstands. Heads turned and eyes stared as I transferred out of my chair and onto the steps and bumped midway up the grandstands to our seats. Fortunately, everyone nearby was patient and when I finally arrived in my seat I received a standing ovation from those who watched my ascent. One minor detail I had forgotten, but I soon realized my oversight. On the parade laps everyone stands up for the race. I had a great view, but it was of everyone's backside. Fatigue and heat got the best of me and we left midway through the race, but I had made it to the race, achieving another of my early goals.

Indian Creek

I was back to cooking lunch at one of our favorite spots—Indian Creek Campground in the Smoky Mountains.

Every summer since 1972 I had traveled to Indian Creek in the Smoky Mountains to fish for rainbow trout. I was determined the summer of 1995 was to be no exception. Our objective for this trip was fishing and camping. By now I had a customized van with a wheelchair lift and hand controls. In years past, we had made the drive to the mountains in one day, but I didn't have the strength this year so we planned a stop midway in Georgia. When making reservations I learned that most handicapped rooms only have one bed. The problem was finding a handicapped-equipped room with two beds. Thanks to the accommodations at the Holiday Inn we were able to travel like any other family.

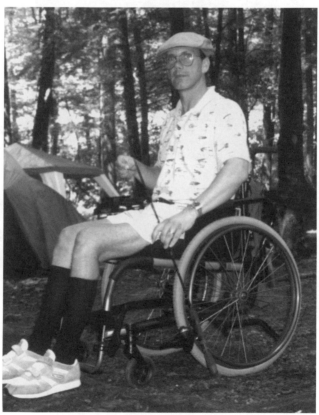

Maneuvering my wheelchair to the stream was not easy, but I managed to catch a couple of rainbow trout.

Our first night on the road was another eye-opener. After checking in, we did what many other traveling families do on a hot day. We headed for the pool. I rolled my wheelchair to the edge of the pool and transferred out of my chair into the water. After several minutes we

By January 1996 I was progressing quickly from my November 1995 surgery in Houston. (Above) I was able to get around with a walker.

(Right) From a homemade standing device, I work on my balance and free throws with Allen.

noticed that most of the people in the pool had cleared out. *Nawww,* I thought, *it could not be me.* But I mentioned my observation to Devon and she had noticed the departure also. When I got out of the pool, other swimmers soon reentered. When I got back in, they left again. I am not contagious, just paralyzed.

Finally we arrived. We stayed in a tiny cabin near the creek. Although our cabin was not wheelchair-accessible, we had a wonderful time. As a family we were reclaiming our place again and a trip to the mountains was the perfect place to begin.

Discrimination Happens

My experience at the motel swimming pool was just one of many similar incidents that have occurred, making me keenly aware of how people with disabilities are often treated differently. For example, it was not uncommon when dining in a restaurant for a waiter or waitress to ask someone other than me at my table what I wanted to eat. Were they going to let me order from the children's menu and bring me a bib as well?

One afternoon while I was shopping in the local Wal-Mart, a young child ran into my wheelchair. The child's mother scolded her, saying, "Watch out for that retarded man." Recently, I sat unnoticed, as other clients were acknowledged, in the lobby of my stockbroker's office. By then I was using crutches, but many people look beyond persons with disabilities. They do not notice us or they avoid us.

I don't harbor bad feelings toward anyone for their reactions around the disabled. More and more of us are surviving terrible accidents thanks to good medicine and smart doctors. Rehabilitation, such as is done at Shepherd, makes it possible for people with disabilities to return to their homes and communities in society and retake their places. I know the situation for us will continue to improve with time. There was a time when African Americans had separate "but equal" facilities and in some places mothers were not permitted to nurse in public. Those prejudicial situations have changed or are improving and so will the problems disabled people have upon reentering society.

I had already been told I was "half a man" by my business partner, so not much else could bother me after that. I can't begin to know what it might be like to be treated differently because of the color of my skin, but I do know what it is like to be treated differently because of my disability. Actually I have come to consider this disability as a gift from God because it has opened many doors and has given me a special insight into discrimination.

C**HAPTE**R 14

My Date with Houston Nears

I'm not afraid of the storms, for I am learning how to sail my ship.
—Louisa May Alcott

When summer came to an end and the kids went back to school, I turned my focus toward surgery. This would be a make-or-break event on my road to recovery and I was determined to be in the best possible condition. I changed my diet, developed an exercise program and prayed for a successful outcome. I made a couple trips to the blood bank to stockpile blood. Knowing the seriousness of the operation I even made my funeral arrangements. Because I was going to be on the operating table for eight hours, I didn't want Devon to be burdened with making arrangements if something went wrong.

I liked the old system of checking into the hospital the night before surgery. I'm sure it kept some patients from going AWOL at the last minute. The prospect of another long surgery was unsettling. If I had not been in so much pain and wasn't so determined to walk again, I might have been tempted to skip town.

I flew to Houston several days before surgery for some final tests and Devon arrived the afternoon before my operation. She was unpacking at the hotel when I returned from the medical center, and over dinner I shared the latest reports from the doctors.

Although I did not have to fast until 9:00 P.M. I started early because I had learned from my research that my postoperative recovery would be easier if I cut off my food intake earlier. My stomach was already full of butterflies so I didn't want much to eat anyway.

November 1, at 5:15 in the morning, Devon and I were in a taxi headed for the Texas Orthopedic Hospital. I was not Superman, but I wished I could be like him and leap tall buildings in a single bound and fly away. When I arrived at the hospital, I called my friend, Fred, and talked about old times. With optimism I said, "See you later this evening."

I already missed my kids and longed to see them.

Not long after we arrived the anesthesiologist paid me a visit. He knew I was uneasy and offered me a cocktail, medical-style. Within a few minutes everything seemed better and I was on my way to surgery. *Boy is it ever cold in here*, I thought, as I was moved off the gurney onto the operating table. I was lying there face up, since they were going through my belly, and looking up at the bright light when the anesthetic took effect and I "went under." The thoracic surgeon began his task of delicately cutting along the lines of my abdominal muscle lines and prepared a work site for the team to do their work.

The operation was a dramatic success and within three months of therapy I was taking my first real steps in public. Devon and I celebrated by going with friends to one of the local restaurants for lunch. At lunch we started talking about our plans to hike to Grinnell Glacier. I was exhausted after just a few steps, but I was walking. The real therapy was about to begin. Countless hours of pain and sweat were my constant companions as I made plans to go to the glacier.

Call Me a Risk Taker

Within three weeks of my miracle surgery in Houston, it was time to achieve one of my goals—to get back in the woods and go hunting. Thanksgiving weekend would be the perfect time. For years Devon, the children and I would go to our hunting camp in Bunnell, Florida, for the long weekend to relax and hunt.

We arrived just before noon to open up our trailer and to get everything in order for our guests, Tom Chase and his boys. Tom and I had hunted together since we were in junior high school, and we were not going to let my injury or recent surgery interfere with our tradition.

It was getting close to time to leave for the woods and Tom had not yet arrived. Wheelchair or not, the decision was easy. I had often hunted by myself in the past and I would go hunting alone. I told Devon where I would be and instructed her to send Tom to another part of the woods so we would not disturb one another. As I was leaving, I said to her, "Don't worry about me if I'm late. I will probably stay and watch the stars rise."

I made my way to the van, rolled the wheelchair on its chair lift and off I drove to the woods—wonderfully independent after all these months.

Devon and I enjoy the family outing at our hunting camp near Moccasin Slough. It gave me a chance to test my independence in the woods.

First I went through the pasture and then into a thicket of pines where I came to Moccasin Slough. A slough is a swampy area with a hard bottom that can hold shallow water. The hard bottom, even covered by water, is solid enough to support a vehicle without using four-wheel drive. I didn't have a problem as I wove and bounced my way along the logging road through another slough after which I found a place to park in the palmettos and pines so my van was concealed.

I rolled in my wheelchair through the woods and stopped along a tree line overlooking another pasture.

This was great. I could hear the wind in the tall pines, a cool wind blowing from the north. I got a whiff of an odor that reminded me that I was in an area that was frequented by cows. In the eastern sky a hawk circled and called out as if it were lost. A group of "rogue gobblers" (mature wild turkeys) marched cautiously to a canal that ran along the far tree line and, one by one, they flew to the safety of their lofty evening roost. That was my signal to head back to camp. I did not see deer, but the glory of hunting is in enjoying everything nature has to offer. The shadows were laying their night sheet across the pasture, as I rolled back to my van. I wondered if my hunting buddies had arrived. I thought, *They are going to be so impressed by my solo venture into the woods*. I was proud, so I figured they would be also.

As I drove back through the slough I felt an unsettling bump and upward lurch. I knew right away I had "high-centered" my van on a cypress knee and was stuck. From the steering wheel I tried every trick I knew to free the van. I was stuck and there was no budging the van until it could be pulled by another vehicle. Camp was a long way off and it was now dark. There was nothing to do but roll in my wheelchair back to camp—a distance of 1.6 miles. While in my chair, I lowered myself on the lift, but the lift would not go all the way to the ground. Another cypress knee was strategically located underneath the lift, blocking its downward movement.

The only way I could get out of the van was to transfer out of the chair and lower the chair over the side of the lift to the ground. No big deal, it was not difficult. I carefully worked myself back into the chair and closed the lift and door by remote control. Everything went smoothly until this point. This part of the slough held fifteen to twenty-inches of water. It was not deep enough to cause a problem for a two-wheel drive vehicle, but it was extremely difficult to navigate in a wheelchair. *Keep your cool*, I thought. *I'll get out of the chair and pull myself and the chair up to higher ground and head back to hunting camp*. It was dark, cool and wet. I was sitting up to my nipples in water, now wondering how I was going to explain being soaked and missing a 4,000-pound vehicle to everyone back at camp.

Upon reaching the water's edge I pulled myself into my chair and started rolling down the old logging road. This was definitely not the adventure I planned to share back at camp. My surgical wound was still healing, and here I had plopped myself into murky swamp water that had been adorned with what cows do after eating grass and chewing cuds all day. Besides, I was in pain from all the activity. Nonetheless, I pushed on. After attempting to roll a few feet—an effort worthy of any Iron Man competition— I knew I was in more trouble.

Me, my chair and this logging road were engaged in mortal combat. The road won and my only means of return was to sit on the ground and drag myself and my clumsy chair backwards along with me. After nearly an hour I arrived at my point of the first slough— Moccasin Slough.

It did not get its name by accident. The slough was usually patrolled by the overweight, foul-tempered, aggressive snakes known

My underwear shows the beating it received as I dragged myself and my wheelchair on my behind as I struggled to get out of the slough.

99

as cottonmouth water moccasins. These snakes are poisonous. As I approached the area where the rough road turns to hard sand, I rolled the last five yards or so to the edge of the water. *Gosh I wish I had a flashlight. Then maybe I could assess the situation.*

How many snakes are there? I wondered. It was not uncommon to see several slithering around when we drove through the slough. Holding my breath, I sat as still as I possibly could, listening and looking. I inhaled slowly and deliberately through my nose trying to pick up the musky odor of the water moccasins. They have a distinctive musky odor, which once you have identified, you never forget. I took another deep breath, nothing. I had no choice. If I wanted to get to camp I had to lower myself into the water. There was no moon and the night was pitch-black. As I settled in the water, I heard a hissing sound. Moccasins make a noise like that as a warning. I made an impossible leap, back into my chair, pulling my legs up one at a time so I could sit cross-legged. My heart was coming up through my throat and pounding its way out of my ears. Without feeling in my lower body, I was not sure where the snake had bitten me.

I knew I had to stay calm and get back to camp to summon medical assistance. I remembered what I had said to Devon, before I left, "Don't worry if I am late. I might watch the stars."

It was possibly too early for her to be alarmed by my failure to return. I worked my way out of the chair and back down to the ground. The snake had not left and was hissing at me again. Out of desperation I just laid my head back on the seat of my chair, looking upward through the canopy of trees and asked, "Why me?" The hissing was louder and closer.

You idiot! You idiot! The source of the sound became clear. My seat cushion was made of a special foam material and when I got out of the chair, it reinflated itself. There was no snake, just the sound of my cushion doing its job. Relieved and feeling a bit foolish, I pulled my wheelchair behind me and I scooted on my backside again through Moccasin Slough as quickly as possible. Two and a half hours after I began my journey, I was greeted by my wife and children who had not yet missed me. They thought I was looking at the stars. I got a cell phone when I returned home.

CHAPTER 15

If It Is Worth Dreaming,
It's Worth Doing

Impossibilities vanish when a man and God confront a mountain.
—Robert Schuller

More than two years had passed since Devon and I sat in the chapel at Shepherd and shared with one another how God had revealed to us shortly after my accident that I would recover and one day walk again. By the summer of 1997, I *was* walking with the aid of Canadian crutches—the kind President Franklin Roosevelt, a polio victim, used when he stood up. I also wore light ankle braces called AFOs (ankle foot orthosis). The time was approaching for me to hike up Grinnell Glacier.

Impractical plans can only be made practical if you are practical people. I like to think Devon and I fall into the category of practical people. In therapy, one area not covered was that you would not only lose the use of your extremities, but you would also lose your "stuff." As a result of my accident we had lost almost every material thing we had worked for so far. A cross-country trip to Grinnell Glacier, miles away, in Glacier National Park in Montana, seemed out of the question. However, we had some money in our savings account and had settled the lawsuit out of court.

Devon and I patiently searched the classified ads and finally found a used twenty-one-foot travel trailer that fit our budget. We bought it, agreeing with one another to sell the trailer upon our return, and began planning an eight-week trip to see America. I knew we had endured some challenges since my accident, but now we were going to really be put to the test. Picture a family of four driving during the day and at night piling into a twenty-one-foot box on wheels to rest and relax. It was truly a wonderful time. We vowed not to eat out during the trip and calculated our additional fuel expenses would run between $900 and $1,200. One of the benefits we discovered was a disabled person could stay in many state and national parks for free or at a nominal cost.

The Higginbotham's home sweet home on wheels.

On June 9, 1997, we packed up, hitched up and headed westward on a trip that would cover nearly 12,000 miles.

Our travels took us through the Smokies then west to the Badlands, through Yellowstone National Park, as far north as Banff and down the West Coast to San Francisco before we headed home. During our last two nights we stayed in a New Orleans KOA. It was a suitable way to end our journey because New Orleans had been our overnight stop when we drove to Houston for that first meeting with the surgical team that put me back together.

We did pretty well with our family vow not to eat out, breaking down only once in San Francisco and twice in New Orleans. We fell in love with our old travel trailer and didn't sell it upon our return home. For me, it is still a comfortable and convenient way to travel. Besides, we don't need to worry about finding a handicap-accessible hotel room and pay extra for the children.

It's a shame I had to break my back to see America, but, oh, what a beautiful and wonderful country we have.

The Trip's Goal

This trip had a special mission. At last I was going to hike to Grinnell Glacier.

Fred and Tammy Johnson, our friends from Plant City, and their three boys, met us in Glacier National Park. During our visit on my first day home from Shepherd, when I confided in Fred that God had told me I would walk, Fred promised that he would make the hike up the glacier with me. It was July 4th and we had our trailer pulled in tight formation with the Johnson family trailer. As evening settled, we could hear the rattling of strings of firecrackers and an occasional hissing of a bottle rocket. In the relatively unpopulated camping area, the only fireworks display that we actually saw was our campfire.

Everyone went to bed except for me. I stayed up late watching a powerful summer storm in the direction of the glacier. After all these months of dreaming and planning and therapy, I couldn't sleep just thinking about the next day and the ascent. For the able-bodied person, the trip is not difficult, but could I make it? What if I failed? I had a sinking feeling, as I knew I had to prove it to myself and to all those who had doubted me. In the morning I would show all those who said I couldn't make it that I would eventually walk again. I was not in denial. I, in Glacier National Park, was about to meet my goal. I was going to the glacier in the morning. I would be the king of the hill. I turned in thanking God for bringing me to this point and I knew if it was His will, I would succeed.

I was the first one up and fixed coffee, eggs, bacon and toast for the two families. But I did not eat or drink anything. Still experiencing problems with my personal plumbing, I knew that the nothing-in-nothing-out method was best for me. I would replenish myself once I made it to the glacier. I didn't talk during breakfast and Fred asked if I was okay. I nodded my head yes.

An hour later we were leaving the Grinnell Glacier trailhead. Devon came over and took the ultra-light fishing gear from my hand. She said, "You're not going to have time to fish on this trip." No, I did not plan to fish, but having my fishing rod in my hand had been part of my plan—my vision during so many hours of physical therapy, I finally told her.

The Walk

Summertime in Glacier National Park is beautiful. The woods are reawakening, the air cool and fresh, as if it had just rained. The park's season is not set by a calendar date, but rather by Mother Nature. It generally opens in June and closes in early September. Extreme weather conditions are common throughout the summer in the higher elevations and rain in the lower elevations. Even though it was July, the nighttime temperature dropped to the high thirties, and the low forties. The morning of the trip to Grinnell Glacier, along with my fishing gear, I took rain gear and a parka in case we experienced bad weather as we approached the top. And, of course, I had my trusty catheter. Just like the charge card commercial, I never leave home without it.

We started out together, but I soon realized my slow pace was a distraction to the others in our party. I urged them to go ahead. I reassured them I had made this trek before and would be just fine. Devon stayed for a few minutes, but I insisted that she go on ahead and catch the group before they got out of sight. She kissed me on the cheek and quickly joined the others.

Like my first day home, and my first hunting trip, I was glad to be alone. As soon as Devon was out of sight, I stopped and sat down on a rock. The trail was muddy and slick from the storm the night before. I scooped a handful of mud and brought it to my face. The fragrance was refreshing as my mind drifted back to the stepping machine in the therapy clinic. I spent countless hours on the machine with this Montana setting in my mind.

I was humbled by the thought of God's healing powers and knew I was chosen for this new mission in life. As I sat there, I prayed,

As I hiked in Glacier National Park, I discovered that some foot bridges were easier to navigate than others. (Below) I took a rest and had my lunch at Grinnell Lake. I savored the mountain view after all these months of dreaming about it.

Devon, Allen and Kaylon share the adventure of our trip to Glacier National Park in 1997.

giving thanks for answered prayers, and especially for His words as I was pinned underneath that tree. I had a glacier to conquer. It was time to get going.

As I made my way up the trail I began noticing that bear tracks were traversing my path. Down on my hands and knees, I examined them closely. By their size I knew it was a grizzly bear. I could place my entire hand in the paw pad and the claws were large enough in diameter that I could stick my fingers in them. I had no interest in walking up on the guy so I took some "bear bells" from my pack and attached them to my shoes and crutches. An able-bodied person might stand a chance with a grizzly if he could climb a tree fast enough, but in my condition, I would end up as a mid-morning snack.

Back on the trail, I made my way past Lake Josephine and had to cross several streams. One of the bridges was so narrow I scooted across it on my backside. A fall would have landed me in the stream several feet below. I wasn't worried about water moccasins here, just freezing water and bears.

My friend, Fred Johnson, who shared both the dream that I would walk, and the hike itself.

Even though the temperature had risen to the mid-fifties, I was drenched in sweat. With limited return of my legs, walking was an arduous and painful task. *Sweat away*, I thought, *today I am in my element.* I was coming to terms with myself and the mountain. I didn't have the balance to look upward as I stood, but during my rest breaks, I watched as the clouds set against a bright blue sky tumbled over the mountains. I took a tube of sunscreen from my pack and put some on. I knew I was not very far from Grinnell Lake, and the final ascent from the lake to the glacier would be above tree line.

When I arrived at the lake, I noticed that someone had built a snowman and then *whack!* I was hit by a snowball. Allen and Kaylon had been waiting for their slow-moving target. Snowball fights and snowmen go hand in hand, but in July? We gathered on the shoreline of the lake to eat lunch when Fred broke the news to me. The final ascent on the steep switchbacks from the lake to the glacier had been closed by the park ranger due to the heavy snow and ice left by the previous night's storm.

As I looked some 1,400 feet up the side of the mountain, I knew I wasn't going to make it to the top, but inside I also knew that I had reached my goal. Sometimes we set goals and get so caught up in the task that we don't realize we have achieved our objective. The same

Devon had faith during some of our darkest hours that I would go hiking again. She hiked to Grinnell Glacier with me in July 1997.

goes for our prayers and the way God answers them—just like the time in the woods with Alice, when I asked her for pain medication and she offered a prayer. Here today, as I stood on the shore of Grinnell Lake, I knew He had answered our prayers.

There is not a step I take, nor a day that passes, that I don't think about that organ donor who died, leaving me the gift of mobility through his or her femur. I will never know the donor's name, but this person walks with me everywhere.

There is one other person who has given me a gift and walks with me every step. His name I do know, Jesus Christ. He died for my sins and I will walk with Him through eternity.

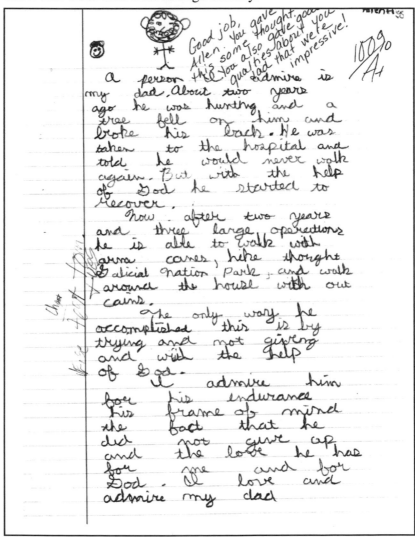

Two years after my accident, Allen received an A+ for his school paper in which he describes it, my recovery, the trek to Grennel Glacier and our family's faith.

CHAPTER 16

After the Mountaintop—the Power of Paralysis

The only disability in life is a bad attitude.— Scott Hamilton

We all face challenges in our lives and make choices. We can be happy, sad, stay down when we are down, accept responsibility or blame others. The choices are clear and simple. It is up to each of us. I know I was at the right place at the right time the day that tree fell on me. It was in God's plan! No, I was not being punished for some misdeed in my life, and God knows I have done them.

Rather, He placed me on a big "time out" to allow me to remake myself and become the man I am today. I know and understand pain, suffering, disappointment and setback. Most of all, I better know myself. And I know with personal faith and His guidance, I can achieve anything I set my mind to. It is no different for you. You make the choice. Can you make the choice? Are you willing to make the choice? Are you willing to pay the price for success? I climbed my mountain.

Through my years in physical therapy I have learned that paralysis is more than just the physical paralysis. There is a paralysis much more serious than mine. It is the emotional and spiritual paralysis from which we all suffer from time to time. I call it personal paralysis. It became very clear to me, as I watched people in therapy, that there were some who had the physical ability to succeed, but their personal paralysis stopped them in their very tracks. Personal paralysis will grab you by your spine and stop you from ever moving forward.

The causes of personal paralysis are many. Sometimes they are accidental, or self-inflicted, and sometimes there is no apparent explanation. During my early days of therapy, as I lay on my workout mat or exercised at a weight machine, I began to identify the causes of personal paralysis.

Fear: Inner fear is the most common form of personal paralysis. It robs you of your self-confidence. So many times success is just over the horizon, or on the mountaintop, but we are unsure and afraid to take the next step. If I stand, will I fall and hurt myself? It is the same in personal paralysis. Are you afraid to make that sales call? Or maybe you have an unresolved problem in a relationship and you don't know how the other party will react to what you plan to say or do.

Bitterness: It would have been easy for me to have become embittered with my circumstances and simply quit trying. I could have blamed others or I could have blamed God for such an unexpected and freak accident and the resulting injuries. Bitterness is a very subtle cause of personal paralysis. Many times we don't even realize we are bitter. Bitterness is like a cancer. It will consume you and eat away at your positive attitude. It will spread and affect others in our lives. Just imagine if I had blamed others for my problems. What a terrible example I would be for my children if I spent my time trying to assign blame. Do you suffer from personal paralysis caused by bitterness?

Anger: In many ways anger goes hand in hand with bitterness. Anger can be caused by bitterness. Again, I could have become angry with God or the events surrounding the hunting trip. Or maybe I could have become angry with the landowner where we were hunting, or one of my hunting companions. We all have experienced someone or have been with someone who angers easily, drives away others, and never accomplishes his or her objectives. Anger is the least desirable cause of personal paralysis.

Jealousy: There were times when I was tempted by jealousy. It was then and still is easy for me to look at someone with greater mobility than mine and become discouraged by jealousy. I have to remember that the past is permanent and nothing can be done to change it. However, it is wonderful to know that my future is waiting for me to determine. Your future is waiting for you to arrive.

Stubbornness: Winston Churchill summed it up best when he said, "I am always willing to learn, although I do not always like being taught." There were many times during my recovery, whether in the hospital at Dothan, the Shepherd Spinal Center in Atlanta, or going through therapy in Plant City that I did not like the suggestions or messages, and sometimes I did not care for the messenger. I wanted to walk again and knew I had to follow instructions. Keep in mind, there is a major difference between determination and stubbornness. I witnessed too many people in physical therapy who were determined to do it their way and never reached the objective. You no doubt have been in a relationship where stubbornness ruled and nothing was ever accomplished.

Guilt: I could easily look back on the day I had my accident and *still* become overwhelmed by the fact that I had neglected my family by going away on another hunting trip—even if the trip was with a business partner. Maybe it is a grievance or misdeed you have committed towards another and you feel there is no way to reconcile your mistake. Remember the past is permanent, but you choose to determine your future.

Pride: There is not a person alive who has not been faced with an issue in which pride has kept him from moving forward. The cause of personal paralysis is often the result of our pride. Think back in your the relationships you have with others or maybe even God. Oftentimes it is pride that prevents us from asking for forgiveness and maybe even forgiving.

How are you handling personal paralysis? Do you blame others? Are you blaming God? Are you masking problems with drugs or alcohol? Are you denying there is a paralysis?

Like a physical paralysis, personal paralysis can lead to anxiety, depression, atrophy—a withering of one's self. It affects the relationships you have with others, yourself and God. But there does not need to be an unhappy ending.

You can overcome your personal paralysis just as I have overcome my physical paralysis. Listen to a few of the steps I followed as I fought back to reclaim my body and myself. The steps are very similar for resolving personal paralysis.

Face the facts and accept responsibility. Yes, face the facts and accept the responsibility. Too often we want to assign the responsibility. I was never in denial, but I had to be realistic about my condition and the environment. I had to learn to take charge of my problems. Many times we turn the burden over to someone else. I am not referring to God in this situation. But, I knew my body better than any nurse or doctor and demanded and expected treatment. You, too, will find the best way to resolve your personal paralysis.

Learn everything there is to know about your problem. Today I am an expert on my spinal cord injury. Ask questions and become familiar with your situation and don't take any detail for granted. Knowledge is power and when you are dealing with a problem affecting your personal growth, it pays to study the problem and handle it before it becomes more difficult to fix.

Find a mentor. No doubt someone has already walked your seemingly lonely path. While still at Dothan, I told my family I wanted some books on a politician who had back and/or mobility problems. I was brought books on Presidents Kennedy and Roosevelt. No, no, I objected—I want a Republican role model. Thus, Senator Bob Dole became mine. This may seem like an obvious step to take; however, when we are caught up in the trial of our paralysis often we may overlook the obvious. You don't think anyone wants to spend time talking and sharing how they overcame a similar problem you now face. You will be surprised.

Stay focused. Okay no big deal, but with me the dynamics of fusion failure, pain and doubt and uncertainty could have thrown me off track. It is so easy to let side issues, even though they are serious, cloud your vision and keep you from resolving your personal paralysis.

It is okay to feel unsettled when resolving your personal paralysis. Remember, the past is permanent and the future is yet to be determined. You may feel you can't put the pieces back together again. You think your issues, once resolved, will never be the same. Well true, they never will be, but that doesn't mean you are not delivered from your personal paralysis. On that day as I lay beneath the tree I prayed to God for a second chance. My prayer was answered and I knew I would live and one day walk again. I will never be the same. Look at me today. Do you see a whole man or a half man broken by paralysis? I walk with crutches and have to wear braces, but I know I am healed and whole.

I have climbed my mountain. I invite you to climb yours.

Epilogue

I never behold them (the heavens filled with stars) that I do not feel I am looking in the face of God. I can see how it might be possible for a man to look down upon the earth and be an atheist, but I cannot conceive how he could look up into the heavens and say there is no God.
—Abraham Lincoln

This book is about overcoming a tragic accident and learning the *real power of paralysis*. It can put you down or pick you up.

The power of my paralysis drives me to push harder, reach higher and achieve more than I did before my accident. Not only did I return to my outdoors activities, but I also used the time while in recovery to return to the world of state and national politics, which I have enjoyed most of my adult life.

Within ten weeks of my accident, I attended the Lincoln's Day dinner, and was honored for my service to the Republican Party. Soon thereafter I was asked to serve as the Hillsborough County, Florida, chairman for Jeb Bush gubernatorial campaign. After that successful campaign, I worked as a regional director in the George W. Bush presidential campaign.

I have looked to many people for motivation and guidance during my recovery. Senator Bob Dole was my role model. He endured a terrible wartime injury, countless hours of agonizing therapy and recovery. His physical limitations did not stand in the way of his success. The following pages of photographs record some special moments during the various state and national campaigns.

*Texas Governor George Bush during presidential campaign, March 2001,
with me and Florida Governor Jeb Bush.   Robert Hartley Photography*

*I am proud to share the podium with my role model, former Senator
Robert Dole.*

Senator Bob Dole and I confer before a political rally in December 2000.

1998 gubernatorial candidate Jeb Bush and I await introduction before taking our places on the stage.

I share a moment with presidential candidate George W. Bush during his campaign.

The Higginbotham family is on its way to the January 1999 Florida gubernatorial celebration.

Mechanics of a Spinal Cord Injury

We tend to forget that happiness doesn't come as a result of getting
something we don't have, but rather of recognizing and appreciating
what we have.—Frederick Koening

Throughout my life I harbored a private fear of paralysis and wheelchairs. Whenever I had seen someone in a wheelchair I avoided them. Were they going to say or do something that required my response? I did not know how to react to someone who was mobility impaired and I knew I could never cope with such a disability. I had decided long ago that I could never survive life as a disabled person. Wheelchairs were for other people. What an awakening I received.

Life is always full of challenges and problems, but I always knew God would get me through the tough times. Life after January 20, 1995, was not going to be an exception. Part of my fear about paralysis and the disability that accompanies it was my lack of knowledge. That is why I think it is important to talk about the mechanics of a spinal cord injury.

The spinal cord is about eighteen inches long and runs through the vertebral column, also referred to as the backbone. The vertebral column consists of thirty vertebrae, divided into the following groups: cervical (C), C 1-8; thoracic (T), T 1-12; lumbar (L), L 1-5; sacral (S), 1-5 and coccygeal 1-4. The sacral and coccygeal vertebrae are naturally fused in adults, and do not move.

When you break a vertebra in your neck or back you will likely end up with spinal cord injury, or nerve damage. It is possible to break or damage the vertebra and not hurt either the spinal cord or nerves. Consider yourself lucky if this happens! The aging process and disease can also damage this sensitive super highway of nerve signals and messages to the body.

Here is a brief outline explaining what body functions are affected by injury to a specific spinal cord level. The brain is the body's central control, with messages transmitted through the spinal cord. A person suffering an injury between C 1-4 may require a ventilator to breathe. C 5, through T-1 send the signals to operate the shoulders, forearms and upper torso. T 2-12 operate the lower torso. L 1-5 control the lower extremities; buttocks, thighs, legs, ankles, feet and toes. Finally, S 1-5 shares some duties, but also controls the bowel, bladder and sexual functions. This is a very basic description of the spinal cord's assignment of duties.

Spinal cord injuries can result in hemiplegia—paralysis on only one side. If you break your neck, everything from the neck (C 1-7), and everything below can be affected. The term used is quadriplegic or "quad. "A broken back (T 1-12, L 1-5, S 1-5) can result in loss of the torso and lower extremities commonly called paraplegic or "para."

Other terms commonly used are: injury level; complete and incomplete injury. Injury level refers to the specific area where you have suffered a spinal cord injury (SCI). Generally a function is affected in the area below your injury level. "Complete" means that no signals make it through the injury level. A complete spinal cord injury does not necessarily mean the spinal cord is severed, but still no signals get through. Often the swelling in and around the spine causes the damage. "Incomplete" means that some signals get through the injury level. However, this signal may be so weak that it has little or no effect on helping your muscles work.

Additionally, you have motor and sensory nerves. It is possible to have sensory loss, but normal motor function, or loss of motor with normal sensation.

Initially, my paralysis involved a complete shutdown of everything from the waist down. My left foot has some sensation (mostly pain) and the right foot has no feeling other than pain. I am deliberate with each step because I don't know where or how my feet have settled.

I can drive a car without the use of hand controls, but feel more comfortable using them since I don't know whether my feet are going to work the gas pedal or brakes. I would not even think of driving a car with a clutch any more.

Other effects of a spinal cord injury may include low blood pressure, inability to regulate blood pressure effectively, reduced control of body temperature, inability to sweat below your level of injury and chronic pain.

Now that I am well into recovery from my spinal cord injury, I routinely see a physiatrist, which is not to be confused with a psychiatrist. Some refer to a physiatrist as a rehabilitation doctor. I also see a urologist (from this planet, not an alien), a proctologist, a podiatrist and an orthopedic surgeon. The physiatrist, Dr. David Haddock, is my primary physician. He works with me on pain management and together we watch for any changes and improvements. At the time I began writing the book, six and a half years after my injury, I still detect some slight and subtle return of motor and sensory function.

Although I don't go to physical therapy anymore, it is important for me to stay limber and fit as I anticipate more progress. And one day I know they will find a way to patch up and fix spinal cord injuries, just as they do now with broken limbs and diseased and damaged organs.

About the Author

Allen "Al" Higginbotham Jr., born in Plant City, a fifth-generation Floridian, received a bachelor of science degree in political science at the University of Florida. In 1972, at age eighteen, he joined the congressional campaign for Florida Democrat Bill Gunter and was hired as one of Gunter's aides. He remained on the staff after Gunter was elected state insurance commissioner and treasurer. In 1979 he entered real estate and married Devon Brown. The couple has two children, Allen III and Kaylon Elizabeth. He opened a successful residential brokerage, which he sold in 1991, and returned to Plant City to work in politics and to assist with a family business. He changed political parties and became a Republican, active again at the state and national levels.

Although recovering from surgery and undergoing physical therapy, Higginbotham served as gubernatorial county campaign chairman for now Governor Jeb Bush, and worked as a regional campaign director for the George W. Bush presidential campaign. He was asked to emcee an event in Tampa in 2001when President Bush appeared. He continues his relationship with the governor and president.

He is active in his church, serves on civic and business boards, is an advocate for persons with disabilities and is a national motivational speaker (see www.   n).

www.alspeaks.com